KWANZAA

From Holiday to Every Day

KWANZAA

From Holiday to Every Day

A Complete Guide for Making Kwanzaa a Part of Your Life

Maitefa Angaza

KENSINGTON PUBLISHING CORP.
www.kensingtonbooks.com

DAFINA BOOKS are published by

Kensington Publishing Corp.
850 Third Avenue
New York, NY 10022

All Kensington titles, imprints, and distributed lines are available at special quantity discounts for bulk purchases for sales promotion, premiums, fund-raising, educational, or institutional use.

Special book excerpts or customized printings can also be created to fit specific needs. For details, write or phone the office of the Kensington Special Sales Manager: Attn. Special Sales Department. Kensington Publishing Corp., 850 Third Avenue, New York, NY 10022. Phone: 1-800-221-2647.

ISBN-13: 978-0-7582-1665-6
ISBN-10: 0-7582-1665-3

First Printing: October 2007
10 9 8 7 6 5 4 3 2 1

Printed in the United States of America

This book is dedicated to my husband,
Menshemsaqa Onaje Angaza,
always my loving support
and a great sounding board;
to the wonderful families I'm so blessed to be a part of;
to Mama Kuumba, who so loved Kwanzaa;
and to Andsister, my Triple-A
and all my invisible, yet very evident, support.

Acknowledgments

My sincere thanks go out to all those who shared their time, energy, or information. As the list is extensive, it's fortunate that this book's format makes clear who many of you are and how you've contributed. I hope each of you who are mentioned within these pages knows how much your assistance is appreciated.

I'd particularly like to thank my gem of an agent, Marie Brown; my wonderful illustrator, Jimmy James Greene, for adding immeasurably to this book; my friend Louis Young for looking out; and my editor Selena James. I received various types of assistance from the following people as well as others whose names appear in their profiles: Jitu Weusi, Salima Moyo, Hemamset Angaza, Men-t S-aungkh Heru Angaza, Mten Halsey, Fatou Mbaye, Veronica White, Segun Shabaka, Adeyemi Bandele, Lumumba Bandele, Mteteaji Mlimwengu, Osei Terry Chandler, Tioma Allison, Nazalima Stephanie Durham, Dafuah Henley, Folake Glover, Lisa Price, Brother Kwasi of Headstart Books in London, Aqa Aakhu Mothudi, Omowale Kierstedt, Baba Zaid Haynes, Sasteh Walters, Mignon Grayson Fagains, Lillian Butler and Eddie Robinson of Raw Soul, Mawule Jobe-Simon, Ner Enen Leonard, Oni Crystal Bowser, Osubi Craig, Nu Web Order Designs, Hostivity, Shukuru Sanders, and Ayanna Johnson.

Contents

INTRODUCTION

The objective in writing this book was to share the information and insight I've gained about Kwanzaa over decades of observance, with an emphasis on the clear and practical. In the process, as with all labors of love, the gift has truly been mine. I've come to a much greater appreciation for Kwanzaa and its potential to serve as an inspiration and change-agent for individuals, families, and groups. Delving into the implications of the Seven Principles has deepened my own commitment to live them consciously throughout the year.

I asked myself the questions I thought readers would have, and the answers were revealing—at times, a bit unsettling. I saw there was so much of value in Kwanzaa that I had not put fully to use. But rather than viewing this as yet another thing to do, I became excited about the prospects presented. I hope that readers will agree that making daily-living guidelines based on the principles of Kwanzaa is an invaluable opportunity of which we can all take advantage.

This book is designed to be used as both a treatise and a how-to. It's crammed with straightforward instructions to get newcomers up-and-running and also provides food for thought for veteran observers. Whether you're trying Kwanzaa on for size in the intimacy of your living room or planning a celebration for an organization hosting lots of guests, you'll find detailed yet accessible assistance. A history of the creation of Kwanzaa is provided, as well as an examination of the issues and the myths surrounding the holiday.

I was really excited to reach the woman whose family hosted the very first Kwanzaa in their California home in 1966. Twenty-five million celebrants later, her account of that gathering is a treasure. I was also elated to communicate with a man in New Zealand who shares his annual Kwanzaa celebration with people indigenous to the land.

I also communicated with people in Africa, the Caribbean, Europe, Canada, and across the United States to determine where, why, and how they celebrate Kwanzaa, and most importantly, how they're making the principles manifest throughout the year. One young woman used the principles of Kwanzaa to help reunite siblings estranged through foster care, a man in West Africa created a youth program named "Kwanzaa," an organization in France uses Kwanzaa as a way to reach the children in their community, and a woman in Cleveland has designed a rites-of-passage program for girls around the Seven Principles. These are just a few of the many inspiring examples readers will find here.

After you've been duly motivated, you'll find a number of ideas for putting your own year-round-Kwanzaa commitment into practice. There are small personal steps you can take, as well as things to do with family, friends, or an organization. You'll find action steps related to each of the Seven Principles; these are things you can do once a week or once a month. Lots of contact information is provided in case you'd like to support an organization or initiative that's involved in work you think is important but you're too busy to do.

I've included in this book a directory of locations of public Kwanzaa celebrations across the United States and in several other countries. There are recipes for the feast, including local specialties from Africa and the Caribbean, vegetarian favorites, and some raw food dishes. This book has the greatest number of Kwanzaa songs ever published and includes a pronunciation key for the Kiswahili words related to the observance of Kwanzaa. Also provided are a wide variety of gift ideas, lists of many shops and online stores that are sources for Kwanzaa cards and other items, loads of book titles for gift-giving or personal enrichment, ditto for music and film, and a directory of dance and musical companies that perform at larger Kwanzaa gatherings.

A good amount of space is reserved for guiding readers through the Kwanzaa celebration from planning to completion. Ideas for determining the type of gathering you'd like to have, inviting guests, and decorating your home or a public venue are all shared. You'll also become thoroughly familiar with the elements of the Kwanzaa ceremony, what to do and what to delegate, what you'll need, what to purchase, and what you likely already own.

It's my hope that this book composes a complete resource for celebrating the holiday. I've listed several other Kwanzaa books as well. What's left is for readers to plan, enjoy, and, I hope, benefit greatly.

MAITEFA ANGAZA

KWANZAA

From Holiday to Every Day

KWANZAAFEST
GIVE THE GIFT OF CULTURE

Chapter One
BIRTH OF A GIANT

KWANZAA at forty-one years old remains vibrant and growing in relevance. Throughout North America and in areas of South America, the Caribbean, Africa, and Europe, it's won devoted adherents. In fact, it is said that more than 20 million people across the world now gather with family and friends to light the candles, sing the songs, and rededicate themselves to the life-affirming values at Kwanzaa's core. These values are the Nguzo Saba, or Seven Principles: unity, self-determination, collective work and responsibility, cooperative economics, purpose, creativity, and faith.

Dr. Ron Karenga, widely referred to by the title "Maulana" (which means "master teacher" in the Kiswahili language), is Kwanzaa's creator. He is director of the Kawaida Institute for Pan-African Studies in Los Angeles, California, and the longtime and now retired chair of the Department of Black Studies at California State University Long Beach. Kwanzaa was conceived in 1966, in the wake of the Watts riots of the previous year, when Karenga sought to equip his people with tools of hope. Generations of African Americans had been subject to racist discrimination and its attendant poverty, substandard education, brutality, and overall disenfranchisement. Anger and desperation eventually erupted on city streets nationwide. To help channel this rage into productive, self-engendered action, Karenga founded the Black Nationalist organization. Its members mobilized in the Los Angeles area to expand the political awareness of the people.

Seeking what Karenga termed "operational unity," US also worked along with similar organizations established across the United States and abroad to build institutions, service the community, provide independent schools and rites of passage programs for youth, demand and develop Black Studies programs in colleges and universities, and protest the Vietnam War, among other things.

Dr. Karenga also held the conviction that Black people would do well to explore the rich resources of traditional African culture and ethics in their quest for liberated minds and lives. He created the Nguzo Saba, which would soon after serve as a centerpiece of his Doctrine of Kawaida, a treatise on "tradition and reason." In the Doctrine he called for a cultural revolution to aid in "the thought and practice of freedom." This new way of thinking and acting would serve to oppose all forms of subjugation, Karenga hoped. It would be a vehicle through which people of African descent could continue to gift the world with their unique expressions of humanity.

The Very First Kwanzaa

Imagine that the first Kwanzaa celebration was held in your own living room! Loyce Foucher, now age seventy-two, opened her Oakland,

California, home for a candle-lighting ceremony, and 20 million people followed her suit. Foucher, who went by "Malika" at the time, and her former husband, Bob Bowen, headed the Institute for Black Studies, which hosted a writing group, art shows, and live theater, and Foucher conducted reading and drama workshops for children. The couple's son, Michael Bowen, held up the letter "z" at that first Kwanzaa celebration and appeared on the cover of *Life* magazine at age six as a Young Simba (junior revolutionary in training). Now a member of the Republican Party, he is the founder of the Conservative Brotherhood and a prolific blogger who, interestingly, wages a vigorous and consistent defense of Kwanzaa on his "Cobb Report" blog. He still celebrates the holiday and is raising his own children to know the full meaning of the Nguzo Saba.

Although Foucher and her former husband never joined the US organization, she first met Karenga when she attended his Kiswahili language class at a local high school. She recalls him visiting their home on a few occasions, which likely led to her family's hosting of the Kwanzaa ceremony. Foucher admits that her recollection of the gathering is limited, but a few memories do remain.

"We celebrated in as African a style as we could," she says, "sitting on the floor with low tables. Everyone was dressed in African attire and brought various dishes to make up the menu. We talked about the Seven Principles and lit a candle each night, I think."

Foucher is proud of the impact of her family's work and is philosophical as she looks back. Shortly after that first Kwanzaa, she repudiated the Black Power movement and since then has lived as a devout Christian.

"In my venture into Black Nationalism, my primary search was for truth," she says, "truth that would explain the world to me in a way that made sense."

The gathering at Foucher's home left a lasting impression on a young man she didn't know at the time. Wesley Sikivu Kabaila, raised in Englewood, New Jersey, was a freshman at Los Angeles City College. He remembers going along with his new friends to hear Karenga speak at a local event and was invited to the Kwanzaa gathering. Kabaila would go on to become the vice chair of the US organization, which he left in the mid-1980s. The event that Foucher remembers in simple terms struck the young student as being "elaborate."

"It was a revelation!" he says. "I'd never experienced anything like it. Karenga presided, as well as some of his associates. I think the general idea was centered around the children, to give them something African-centered to do during that holiday season. We never anticipated that it would grow the way that it has."

"Some parents were skeptical" at first, Kabaila recalls. "They weren't certain they wanted their children involved. But as Kwanzaa began to gain in popularity, people identified with it and resonated with its significance. It didn't offend anyone's religious beliefs because it was a cultural holiday. The whole emphasis was on Africa and getting back to our traditions."

Kabaila remained in California, where he attends the Kwanzaa parade each year. He'd like to thank Loyce Foucher and her family for allowing him to play a small part in history.

In the interest of providing a social tool to aid in this reclaiming of African culture, Karenga created Kwanzaa in 1966. Structured around his Nguzo Saba to provide seven principles for living and a celebration rich in significance, it was inspired by traditional harvest festivities. Indigenous Africans across the continent were historically wedded to the land as a source not only of sustenance, but also of identity and inspiration. They would take time at the close of an agricultural season to express their appreciation to the Creator for life's gifts and for one another.

These harvest celebrations varied from place to place, from the Yam Festival of Ghana to the Kambala celebrated by the Nuba people of Sudan. They all involved, however, taking stock of the challenges faced and the progress made by the community, as well as a recommitment to facing the future as a healthy, highly functioning whole. Community members would gather to joyfully share the fruits of their labor. Delicious traditional dishes would be prepared using the produce of the land, and the festive music, dance, and dress were both reward and incentive—a good time could be had by all, if all were willing to contribute. Although many people of African descent no longer grow their own food, Kwanzaa maintains the agricultural reference as more than a metaphor. Ownership of land remains an issue of importance in many Black communities the world over. It is a link to the ancestors of the lineage and a critical factor in the prospects for the future of the people.

Along with the Nguzo Saba, Karenga also identified five fundamental concepts underlying the intent and application of the Kwanzaa holiday. They are not an addendum to the Seven Principles, but a framework that celebrants can use to ensure an authentic Kwanzaa observance. The five fundamentals are:

- Unity of family, friends, and community
- Reverence for the Creator and Creation, encompassing an appreciation of, and respect for, the environment
- Commemoration of the past, which includes honoring one's ancestors and valuing one's heritage

- Commitment to the cultural ideals of the African community, including truth, justice, and mutual respect
- A celebration of the "Good of Life" and appreciation for the blessings of achievement, family, and community

An Ancient Practice Adapted for a New Day

The word "Kwanza" means "first" in the Kiswahili language, which was chosen because it is spoken as either a first or a second tongue by close to 50 million people in Eastern, Central, and parts of Southern Africa. Subtitling his creation "The Celebration of the First Fruits" (Matunda ya Kwanza), Karenga placed an additional "a" at the end of "Kwanza," forming a seven-letter word to resonate with the foundational Seven Principles at the heart of the Doctrine of Kawaida. One former US member, who was present at the very first Kwanzaa celebration, remembers that there was an additional incentive for the extra "a." He says that seven of the members' children were preparing a Kwanzaa presentation and each wanted to represent a letter of the word.

Today Kwanzaa delights millions of children across the globe, and those first celebrants are amazed at the life it's claimed as its own. Karenga has traveled to speak in several foreign countries and shares his founder's message in cities across the nation each year. The National Association of Kawaida Organizations (NAKO) hosts annual Kawaida symposiums on the theory and practice of the doctrine created around the Nguzo Saba. In South Africa, far from its origins but close in application to a traditional Zululand harvest festival, Kwanzaa is observed by longtime celebrants such as music legends Caiphus Semenya and his wife, Letta Mbulu.

Putting His Stamp on Kwanzaa

Artist Daniel Minter is the designer of the second U.S. Postal Kwanzaa stamp, issued in 2004, and his proud, colorful figures have become a familiar sight to many. (The first stamp, issued in 1997, was designed by artist and author Synthia St. James.) Here, in edited form, is Minter's statement on this small work that is large in significance and limitless in exposure potential:

"Two mothers, Imani and Nia, are holding the community together. One is a physical mother, and one a spiritual mother. Both wear crowns of fabric to distinguish themselves and atop each crown is a Sankofa bird [which] looks to the past to understand the present, and never forgets from where it came. They are Kuumba, ready to fly. The other five figures look to the left, the right, forward and back, they look to each other. They are Umoja and Ujamaa. They all wear robes that are blowing in the wind like flags, all moving in the same direction, represent[ing] Kujichagulia.

"The colors red, black, green, gold and yellow represent the continent of Africa. Red is for the blood that we have shed, black is for our people, green is for the land and growth, gold is for wealth and prosperity, and yellow is for the sun, or the future. The blue in the center represents the mother, the source of life, the ocean. When these colors and patterns are displayed together on the stamp panel, they form a quilt of the sort that our mothers and grandmothers made." Find out more online at www.danielminter.com.

The rapid growth of Kwanzaa was due, in large part, to its being promulgated in the 1970s as part of the practice of Kawaida. Members of the Congress of Afrikan Peoples, most notably Amiri Baraka, then of New Jersey's Committee for a Unified Newark, Jitu Weusi of The East organization in Brooklyn, New York, and Haki Madhubuti of the Institute for Positive Education in Chicago, made sure that the word was spread throughout their cities and later across the nation.

There are now all manner of initiatives named after the holiday, such as: A.P.C.K. Kwanzaa, an organization based in Paris, France, that promotes the holiday and its principles; KwanzaaCameroon, the youth-mentoring program in that African nation; Kwanzaa—The Afrikan Shop, a retail outlet with a cultural mission in Aotearoa/New Zealand; and the Kwanzaa Playground in Columbus, Ohio. There are also any number of programs bearing the names of the Seven Principles, including: the Umoja Festival in Portsmouth, Virginia; Kujichagulia Lutheran Center in Milwaukee; Ujima Housing Association of London; Ujamaa School in Washington, D.C.; Nia Comprehensive Center for Developmental Disabilities in Chicago; the Kuumba Singers of Harvard College; and Imani Winds, a New York City–based African American/Latino quintet.

There are children named Nia, Imani, and zawadi, people whose first or last names are Umoja, and a woman named Mama Kuumba, who until her passing in 2004, served as a faithful Kwanzaa ambassador in New York City. Other examples include jazz, R&B, classical and choral compositions, dance troupes, theater companies, lesson plans, antiviolence initiatives, substance abuse prevention programs, holiday expos, a U.S. postage stamp, books, games, dolls, videos, summer camps, and even a lion in a Birmingham, Alabama, zoo. Whatever one thinks of this trend, it's clearly in evidence: all the abovementioned are named for Kwanzaa concepts, with many inspired by, and some devoted to, its principles. A chord has been struck, and its reverberations have stirred communities worldwide.

As Kwanzaa is the celebration of the "first fruits," it's a time to give thanks for the harvest of ideas we've brought to life and the sacrifices we've made in the year now coming to a close. At Kwanzaa time we look within to determine where we are on our life's journey, where we stand in relation to our community, and what we've done to advance those values we hold highest. We do this both singularly, in the sanctuary of our quiet moments, and together with family, friends, and colleagues during joyous celebrations. These private and public reflections help us to set our compasses for the year ahead; although our mistakes may give pause, when contemplating our blessings, we give thanks.

Kwanzaa Greetings from Chicago

Yakini "Charles" Haynes and Kenyetta Giles Haynes, owners of the Ankh juice bar in Chicago, Illinois, have celebrated Kwanzaa for approximately twenty years.

"While we strive to practice the principles as part of our daily existence," says Yakini, "we appreciate setting aside time to reaffirm and rededicate ourselves to a purposeful way of life. We feel happy, blessed, and rejuvenated."

The couple does the candle-lighting ceremony together each evening, makes it a point to send Kwanzaa cards each year, and encourages friends to attend events where they can learn more about the holiday and participate in celebrating it. They enjoy attending several of the week-long events held across the city, particularly those held at their house of worship, the Trinity United Church of Christ, for which, they say, people travel from near and far. The church hosts special guest speakers, has a daily sermon based on the Nguzo Saba, and holds a much anticipated Imani celebration.

The Hayneses will, from time to time, host a gathering at their home for friends, family, and extended family. During the karamu there's lots of laughter, food, and good music in the background.

"We form a unity circle and encourage children to share a cultural expression or make a general statement about a Kwanzaa principle and what it means to them," says Kenyetta.

"Adults and children are invited to read or recite a poem, sing, do a dramatic or interpretive dance," adds Yakini. "At the end we play a few rounds of 'Black Facts' or some sort of African history game for prizes like books, greeting cards, and CDs. Kenyetta's mother, Etta Wheeler Giles, gave us a copy of *The African American Book of Values: Classic Moral Stories* by Steven Barboza a few years ago. It has been an indispensable resource for classic works to share with our guests. We've had some very colorful performances. One year a family member adapted the song 'Teach Me Tonight' for a family audience and applied it to the Seven Principles."

The Haynes family starts the new year infused with the energy gained from a meaningful holiday season.

"We attempt to incorporate the positive energy generated from family, friends, cultural activities, educators, spiritual leaders, lecturers, books, films, music, etc., into what we do and what we feel we are called to do," says Kenyetta. "We try to live in a more balanced, purposeful, and meaningful way." Contact Ankh at (312) 834-0530 or www.ankhlife.com.

I Celebrate Christmas: Why Add Kwanzaa?

Over the years there has been a certain amount of confusion about Kwanzaa's connection, if any, to the Christmas holiday, considering that it begins directly afterward. There was no connection at the time that Kwanzaa was conceived and there remains none. People across the globe have added Kwanzaa to their family's holiday observances, recognizing that as it is not a religious holiday, it does not stand in conflict to the practice of any faith. Nonetheless, this cultural holiday does have spiritual applications, evidenced by Kwanzaa's focus on ethics, self-assessment, and expressions of thanks to the Creator for the "harvest."

Dr. Karenga has said there are several reasons that Kwanzaa is observed as the year draws to a close. One factor is that this period falls in line with several traditional harvest celebrations which predate Christmas and are still observed in parts of Africa at this time of year. One example is Umkhosi, the harvest festival of the Zulu people of South Africa, which is a central model for Kwanzaa. Karenga also noted that most people have some time off from work to spend with family and friends during the winter holiday season. Another benefit was the providing of a focus on values, rather than spending, for communities least able to afford the post-holiday debt.

Although Black Nationalists and Cultural Nationalists were first to embrace and popularize it, people of varying social and political perspectives now celebrate Kwanzaa, some faithfully each year, others casually, when invited to a ceremony. Included among them are people of many faiths and beliefs, including Muslims, Buddhists, Hindus, Yorubas, Akans, Kemetians, Spiritualists, Atheists, Humanists, and Agnostics. They find that Kwanzaa supports their own values by providing an additional formula for acting on them.

Christians are embracing Kwanzaa in rapidly growing numbers each year. Baptists, Methodists, Lutherans, Episcopalians, Catholics, and others are observing at home with their families and with fellow believers in their sanctuaries. The ethics that underpin Kwanzaa have inspired many church endeavors and there are places of worship named for the holiday and its principles. Minneapolis, Minnesota, has two: the Kwanzaa Community Fellowship Church, which has a garden with seven benches representing the Seven Principles, and the Greater Imani Church. In fact, the term "Imani Church" has become somewhat popular; we find houses of worship with this name in Cleveland, Ohio; Austin, Texas; Durham, North Carolina; and Trenton, New Jersey.

Safiyah Fosua of the General Board of Discipleship of the United Methodist Church has seen the holiday grow in prevalence as people of her faith find meaningful ways in which to incorporate it into their celebrations. While some Methodist congregations now observe Kwanzaa as a church family and others invite the public, the use of the Bible remains central, she says, clarifying for congregants those traditional

African values that have a counterpart in Christian spirituality. Illustrating how Methodists can use scripture readings to aid in their reflection on the Nguzo Saba, Fosua cites the examples of Nehemiah 4:6 and 6:15 for Kujichagulia (self-determination), and 2 Kings 2:11–14 for Nia (purpose).

Kwanzaa's emphasis on principles has clearly found favor among many communities of faith and its reach extends into various other arenas of life, as well. In the absence of worldwide media exposure or advertising campaigns, it has made its way into households, classrooms, and public meetings, its maxims being translated into several languages. College students and retirees, social entrepreneurs and corporate executives, old married couples and young singles, new parents and grandparents, now observe the holiday at home with family. Most have also showed up to someone else's Kwanzaa ceremony, with or without a plate of food. They come to sing those Kwanzaa songs and bear witness to the good, their convictions ignited anew with the lighting of the candles.

One of the reasons Kwanzaa has been widely embraced is that it speaks directly to the need many feel for a self-determining way of engaging the world. In observing a holiday created by a man of African ancestry as a contribution to his people and to the world, we claim the hard-won freedoms paid for by the sacrifices of all our forebears. In gathering with like-minded people so that together we might make a greater difference, we exercise the right to congregate often denied some of our ancestors. Language differences and the threat of the lash prohibited enslaved Africans from talking freely among themselves, but as we engage in discussion about the Seven Principles, we honor the ability to openly discuss the direction in which freedom lies. And in playing drums at Kwanzaa gatherings and singing empowering songs, we remind ourselves that these ways of communicating and uplifting our spirits are not to be hidden for fear of reprisal, but celebrated as liberating expression.

Many of the people who celebrate Kwanzaa have never heard of Dr. Karenga and are unfamiliar with the origins of the holiday. They've chosen to embrace a concept whose reach has, for some time now, extended beyond a personality or an ideology. Around the world, the assessment of the people is that Kwanzaa works.

Kwanzaa as a Rite of Passage

In Cleveland, Ohio, each year, a group of teen and preteen girls leads a public Kwanzaa ceremony and then performs for those in attendance at the karamu that follows. Sitting on the side, no doubt beaming with pride, is Sekhmet Nefertari Lee-Ivey, founder of the Safiri Rites of Passage Program. She knows her young women in training are equipped to handle the responsibility because they've been preparing for it.

"Our rites of passage group teaches how to incorporate the Nguzo Saba in daily living," says Lee-Ivey. "Throughout the year the initiates receive seven tests based on the principles; they must all pass or fail together. Our ceremony day varies—one year it may be held on the second day, and the next year on the fifth, and we do Kwanzaa community projects each year to demonstrate that principle. We've collected books for Africa, canned goods for shelters, clothing for men, women, and children, and written letters to family members we haven't communicated with in years."

The initiates make zawadi for the celebration, such as bracelets, potpourri with African cloth, recipe and affirmation books, and lotions. Lee-Ivey stresses the personal impact of a handmade gift. The girls take part in organizing the celebration, including the meal planning.

"Our karamu always features dishes from around the Diaspora," Lee-Ivey continues. "We've made a tradition of passing out recipes for African dishes in advance to those who are regulars at our gatherings. If you're new to Kwanzaa, we ask you to make a recipe passed down through your family. We've also conducted an African naming ceremony, which will become an annual feature." Contact Lee-Ivey about the program at JLeeIvey@mail.ignatius.edu.

Chapter Two

THE SEVEN PRINCIPLES OF KWANZAA

The Names and Definitions

THE Nguzo Saba (Seven Principles) are the foundational ethics that order our thinking in line with Kawaida (tradition and reason). They represent values critical to the building of personal integrity and functional community.

Umoja (Unity)

To strive for and maintain unity in the family, community, nation, and race.

Kujichagulia (Self-Determination)

To define ourselves, name ourselves, create for ourselves, and speak for ourselves.

Ujima (Collective Work and Responsibility)

To build and maintain our community together and to make our brothers' and sisters' problems our problems, and to solve them together.

Ujamaa (Cooperative Economics)

To build and maintain our own stores, shops, and other businesses and to profit from them together.

Nia (Purpose)

To make as our collective vocation the building and developing of our community in order to restore our people to their traditional greatness.

Kuumba (Creativity)

To do always as much as we can, in the way we can, in order to leave our community more beautiful and beneficial than when we inherited it.

Imani (Faith)

To believe with all our hearts in our people, our parents, our teachers, our leaders, and the righteousness and victory of our struggle.

The Significance and Implications

Following are reflections on the significance and implications of the Nguzo Saba. As you prepare to celebrate Kwanzaa, examine your own thoughts on the meaning and broader applications of these Seven Principles. Write them down and add to them each year. This will be invaluable in helping you to make the most of your annual observance.

Umoja

Unity is a fundamental requirement for the progress of a people, an integral component of effective action. It provides a platform for individual growth and collective advancement, while not requiring that we all think or act alike. In fact, mutual respect for the diversity of nationalities, experiences, and ideas represented among a people can only serve to strengthen their bonds. A little willingness and a measure of discipline can aid us as we "strive for and maintain unity in the family, community, nation, and race." Members of a family are more resilient if they can rely upon one another for acceptance and support. A community is made viable when everyone contributes. Nations are more secure when there is open dialogue on policy, and a race of people can better survive adversity if it values commonalities over contradictions.

A Fruitful Kwanzaa in Jamaica

Brother Ireko is the founder and director of Wilderness House of Arts, a community cultural center located in a historic building in St. Mary's Parish in Jamaica, West Indies. Ireko has, since the year 2000, opened the Center's doors to those interested in celebrating a meaningful Kwanzaa, one filled with activities and inspiration.

"My main interest is to educate people," says Ireko. "Christmas occupies the attention of most here, but you also have people who are looking for alternatives and those who are just curious."

The curious leave with food for thought, and regulars are reenergized. Ireko prints leaflets explaining the holiday and will review them at each gathering throughout the week. A local radio station announces the programs, and some people come for a day while others attend all seven. On one day, visitors might take part in a dance workshop;

on others, they'll dialogue with natural health practitioners, be treated to live music or a poetry showcase, take a yoga class, or paint and make crafts under the direction of local visual artists. The idea is that they are together, affirming community and discussing ways in which to uphold the values of the Seven Principles.

"I'd like to see the principles of Kwanzaa become an automatic part of our everyday consciousness," Ireko says. "Christmas became what it is over two thousand years ago and Mother's Day didn't exist once. If we keep persisting, Kwanzaa will grow in the consciousness of the people."

If you happen to be in Jamaica during the Kwanzaa season and are interested in attending a meaningful, modest-sized gathering, the Center's doors are open to those who enter in the Kwanzaa spirit. Contact Ireko at (876) 994-0578.

Of course, Unity is a particularly critical issue for people of African descent, many of whose ancestral families were torn apart during the transatlantic slave trade. The resulting trauma was profound and its residual effects are still evident today, despite incredible achievements in the face of enormous odds. Preoccupation with color, class, or background are milder manifestations of the ideas that lead to fatal conflicts over religious beliefs and tribal heritage in Africa, and gang violence on city streets in the United States. While these are global problems by no means peculiar to people of African descent, it can be argued that we can least afford them. Each person can contribute to the development of greater unity through conscious effort to work in cooperation with others.

Kujichagulia

A self-determining people are an asset not only to themselves, but to the world. In our resolve to "define ourselves, name ourselves, create for ourselves, and speak for ourselves," we assert our freedom of thought and our God-given authority over the direction of our lives. Self-definition is exercising the right to choose our own identity and to decide for ourselves what is essential. When we name ourselves, we claim a basic human right that was denied many of our ancestors: the prerogative to decide what we'll call ourselves and call our children, and what we'll answer to, as well. Creating for ourselves means that we take the initiative to provide what is needed in our own lives and in our communities, rather than depending on these things being supplied by others. In speaking for ourselves, we communicate our own intent and articulate our own terms, while upholding our right to address the world on our own behalf and to be heard.

Rethinking Holidays

Ayo Handy Kendi of Washington D.C. is on a special mission when it comes to holidays. She's drawn a line in the sand that marks what she feels is her right to celebrate what and how she pleases.

Kendi's public involvement with Kwanzaa began in 1981, when she began making presentations on the holiday at area schools.

"I'd travel around to the various independent Black schools, but I began to feel that our children in the public schools were being left out," she says. "Also, an increasing number of people would approach me for information, so I produced a small 'How to Celebrate Kwanzaa Guide.' The next thing you know, I was on local radio and TV! I explained lots of things, like how to break Kwanzaa down to preschoolers with songs and interactive fun."

Kendi believes in getting things started. She founded the African American Holiday Expo in 1982 and, since 1989, has served as founder and director of the African American Holiday Association (AAHA), which "perpetuates and preserves culture through traditional and nontraditional holidays, celebrations, and rituals." Kendi's Youth Entrepreneur Project (YEP) gives young people in her area the skills to make handcrafted items and the opportunity to sell them at seasonal expos. She also founded two commemorative "wholydays," Ancestor Honor Day, and Black Love Day (February 13), which she poses as an alternative to Valentine's Day. She also travels each year telling stories, leading songs, and performing as "Mama Ayo, the Kwanzaa Griot." She feels she's contributing to the reclamation of tradition.

"As a people whose ancestors commemorated holidays and celebrated in a vital way, this is still part of our DNA. We didn't lose everything in the Middle Passage. Today our ancestral memory is coming back and it's providing a chance to heal."

Kendi and the African American Holiday Association can be reached through its Web site, aaha-info.org, where her video, *How a Family Celebrates Kwanzaa,* is offered.

The committed practice of Kujichagulia helps to develop healthy self-regard and a greater appreciation for the rights of others. We focus our attention on creating our own opportunities and meeting our own responsibilities. In remaining accountable, individually and collectively, for the choices we make, we empower ourselves. It is our right to choose what to do with that power. We are fully capable of deciding for ourselves what's in our best interest as persons and as a people, and can require that others respect that right.

A decision to observe Kwanzaa, not seeking the permission or approval of others, is an act of self-determination. To those who question our choice to celebrate a "made-up" holiday, we point out that not only were all holidays made up, but we are practicing Kujichagulia when we create something to satisfy our own needs. We lost the lion's share of our traditions during the enslavement of Africans. Most of us don't know how our ancestors celebrated births or birthdays, weddings or funerals, and we have the right to be creative as they were, establishing traditions that reflect our values.

Ujima

The most direct route to the realization of our objectives is the collective path of action. Access and ability are magnified when we join with others, each applying their own particular talents and perspectives. We can shed greater light and harness optimal inspiration in working together; our thrust forward has more muscle and greater staying power. The joy we often find in collaboration and caring for one another can make light work of our efforts. Everyone benefits when we set out "to build and maintain our community together and to make our brothers' and sisters' problems our problems, and to solve them together."

In building a community, we have the opportunity to contribute to its fundamental framework and to determine where it will best serve us and how. While maintaining our communities, we validate for ourselves, and for the younger generations watching, that we are good caretakers capable of building legacies. Taking more than an idle interest in the challenges faced by our brothers and sisters is actually in our own best interest. The world is a better place for us all if we contribute to making it so by modeling how to be responsive to the needs of others. Each individual decision to be of aid and service to the extent that we can infuses hope, vitality, and strength into the collective body that is the people.

Ujamaa

Economic power, while not the ultimate reality underpinning our existence, does weigh heavily on the scale of imperatives in today's world—a world created by prevailing ideas about money. We can view the acquisition and distribution of money from a self-centered perspective or consider it in a broader context, where how we earn and spend money has meaning beyond ourselves. If we look at our earning and accumulating potential as economic power, then we cannot feign ignorance of how that power is used, or to what effect. Responsible persons should know whether or not their hard-earned cash or carefully considered investment is enriching their community and the people they turn to for support when needed.

Kwanzaa: A Store and More in New Zealand

Lewis Edward Scott, owner and operator of Kwanzaa—The Afrikan Shop in New Zealand, has nursed the Kwanzaa flame in an area where few are familiar with the holiday. An African-American poet and writer born in Cordele, Georgia, Scott has lived in his adopted home for several years and refers to it by its original name, Aotearoa/New Zealand.

Not surprisingly, Kwanzaa—The Afrikan Shop, at 119 Manners Street in Wellington, has been centrally involved in increasing awareness of Kwanzaa in the country. Scott enjoys using the store in the spirit of Umoja, and as his own family is back at home in the United States, it's helped him to create a communal zone. In his words, he's seeking to "facilitate political and social interaction between the African/African-African community and the indigenous people of color."

"I host guest speakers and various events such as poetry readings," says Scott, "and generally try to make contact with any African-Americans visiting Aotearoa/New Zealand to create a home-space for them."

Scott's Kwanzaa celebrations are eagerly anticipated. The small African/African-American community relishes the opportunity to gather, and Scott's Maori, Aborigine, and Pacific Islander friends indigenous to the region love being invited to participate. Scott travels to Africa once each year, visiting various countries over two to three months. Items he's obtained there are carried in the shop as Kwanzaa gifts. Guests do bring dishes to the karamu, but you won't find any collard greens or candied yams. On the menu is local produce, such as kumara and taro, puha greens, and watercress, which may be served along with kina (sea eggs) or other traditional favorites. The Kwanzaa celebrations help Scott fill his own appetite for progressive community.

"Politically and socially, I'm a product of the sixties and I've celebrated Kwanzaa for many years," says Scott. "As an individual and a businessman who is aware of the social and political aspirations of the people of color in this part of the world, I strive to conduct my business and personal life around the Seven Principles of Kwanzaa." Readers can contact Scott and Kwanzaa—The Afrikan Shop at sunflower@actrix.co.nz.

In order to "build and maintain our own stores, shops, and other businesses and to profit from them together," we need the caring and clarity of mind required to make wise choices. In patronizing our own businesses we profit together. As they thrive, our ability to "do for self" increases; with enlightened interdependence we reduce our dependency on the resources of others or on government aid. It begins with a willingness to take that first, most basic step: going out of our way to spend our dollars where it counts toward our community's benefit.

Nia

If we are to "make as our collective vocation the building and developing of our community in order to restore our people to their traditional greatness," we must first admit that most of us are unfamiliar with the concept of a "collective vocation." If I have no interest in that which highly motivates you, am I expected to subordinate my own objectives? The answer is no. Nia does not require that we sacrifice our unique vision or the pursuit of our life's purpose. It does, however, involve identifying those bottom-line fundamentals we have in common, such as the right to compete fairly for opportunities and the room to grow our families, businesses, and organizations without threat from hostile individuals or institutions.

When we recognize the common challenges we face, it is a natural response to join together to better address them, just as residents in a coastal community will work together to board up everyone's windows. We don't have the option to declare the difficulties we face too great to overcome. In the absence of that luxury, we become people on a mission; in other words, we have a collective vocation. While one person pursues a career in dentistry and another in dance, both can lend support to those advocating for safe streets, for example. The building and developing of our communities becomes a more viable prospect when we are clear about the need to work together. In fact, we should consider it a privilege to collaborate with one another; we are people who have proven to be among the world's most humane and resilient citizens. Given our character, safeguarding our legacies and realizing our potential are achievable goals with hard work and unified focus.

Staying Principled in Pennsylvania

Denise Hinds-Zaami, who lives in the town of State College, Pennsylvania, has celebrated Kwanzaa for thirty-five years. Although she's observed at work, at her son's school, and with friends, small groups, and organizations she's been with, she looks forward to the intimate candle-lighting ceremony at home each evening with her only child, her son, Mahdi. She doesn't live close to family, but extended family are sometimes involved if they are around.

"Here at Penn State University, where I work, The Black Graduate Students Association regularly hosts a Kwanzaa event, which is open to the public, and I attend," says Denise. "When I was president and a member of The New York Association of Black Psychologists, we held an annual Kwanzaa event, which was always open to the public."

Denise and Mahdi make their gifts to one another, and they've exchanged food, pictures, wood-works, and their favorite—books. They've also bought books related to Kwanzaa and its principles and sent them to family members in the United States and abroad as well as to people they don't know who don't have much. Mother and son usually exchange gifts on the first day of Kwanzaa, rather than the last. Denise feels that children, who so anticipate gifts, shouldn't have to wait too long. She also wants the gift associated with the Winter Solstice, which occurs December 21 through 24. One of the things Denise contemplates during the solstice is how she'll bring the Nguzo Saba to life in the upcoming year.

"I do take steps to practice the Seven Principles throughout the year," says Denise. "I also try to teach my son to do so, and to share my attempts to do so with others. For Umoja, I try to remain focused on my commitment to our people and participate, with every opportunity, in events which uplift us as a group and give us life. For Kujichagulia if I decide I want to do something, I move towards getting it done.

"For Ujima I have founded The Moveable School, a collective of parents who want to be involved in the education of their children. It's not a school which has a building; it meets every few months, rotating presentations and presenters.

"For Ujamaa, I try to 'Buy Black' whenever I can. For Nia, I again try to remain focused and not let what I want for my person, my family, and my people out of my conscious awareness. I live Kuumba daily, as I love to do anything that I do with my own creative flair. And for Imani, I pray daily in an elaborate way (mostly at meals). I take many risks and also enjoy traveling to many lands (last year my son and I were in Antarctica). One must have faith in order to do these things."

Kuumba

Creativity has been the lifeblood of our people: it's brought us along and held us up during times when nothing else could. On those occasions when we feel that faith has failed us, creative thinking can help us to find our way back to it. Our creativity has been used to make our lives pleasurable and to better our own conditions, even resulting in the establishing of world-famous figures in the arts, in business, and in a host of other fields. It's changed and beautified the world and often, in the absence of access or initiative on our part, made wealth-producing industries for others. Such a powerful force should be respected and used with the utmost care to make life a more glorious experience for all. Never should we condone it being exploited to justify inhumanity or to create slavish markets for demeaning fare.

Kwanzaa with My Father, Yusef Iman

Malika Iman is the daughter of a revered figure of the Black Arts Movement who joined the ancestors years ago and far too soon. Yusef Iman was a poet, playwright, director, actor, and cultural nationalist entrepreneur. His original Kwanzaa songs and theatrical productions played a significant role in popularizing the holiday on the East Coast. Malika is a longtime dancer and author of the book *Intimate with the Ultimate: Memoirs and Tribute to Family, Cultural, Political and Spiritual Activism,* in which she travels down memory lane to give readers a sense of her father and the unique way in which her family spent Kwanzaa seasons.

"When the holidays came around we were the most active of all families. Besides going over to my grandparents' for Thanksgiving and Christmas to eat to our hearts' content, we also traveled to do what seemed like *non-stop* performances for Kwanzaa! My father was literally considered the 'Kwanzaa Man' on the East Coast.

"Kwanzaa starts on December 26, however, we were overwhelmingly booked for pre-Kwanzaa shows to teach about how to celebrate and practice the holiday. My father made it easy for everyone to understand. As my brothers drummed, my sister, mother, and I would come out dancing with the Kwanzaa items. He'd call the name of each, have the audience repeat it, and then elaborate on it. He would sing the Nguzo Saba in English and in Swahili, using our traditional way of 'call-and-response' and would explain the principle for each day and what should take place.

"Although Kwanzaa was very new it was graciously accepted because we made it a totally interactive and fun experience for audiences. My father also wrote, and sang in his rich bass/baritone voice, a beautiful and melodic song about Kwanzaa and its cultural significance.

"We were always on a roll, with non-stop, bona fide Black 'Inner-Attainment.' We worked at many different venues throughout the nation. Sometimes, it was five or six shows a day! *This was work!* Nevertheless, we got through it because we loved sharing and being the cultural pathway for our people to proudly dance through." You can reach Malika at (212) 252-3907 or find out more about *Intimate with the Ultimate* at malika3939@yahoo.com.

If we are to "do always as much as we can, in the way we can, in order to leave our community more beautiful and beneficial than when we inherited it," we must be committed to the productive use of creativity as a people and as individuals. Doing as much as we can means pushing past what feels comfortable to arrive at what's possible; oftentimes creativity can be employed to expand the perception of the possible. Just as we make art in our own living rooms, we can build art institutions together. That idea you came up with to salvage the family finances could, if replicated, save a community. Doing things in the way we can allows us to approach matters from our creative perspectives and to make art informed by that vision and those objectives. We create more beautiful and beneficial communities when we are open to one another's ideas. If we're willing to listen to our best creative thinkers, we can utilize the creative capital we've been granted to conceive more innovative communities and to claim our place on the global stage.

The Kwanzaa Queen

It's difficult for Salima Moyo to remember a time growing up when she wasn't celebrating and loving Kwanzaa. Her family, her extended family, and her schoolmates at Brooklyn's Uhuru Sasa Shule all helped to make cherished memories of a special week of gatherings, good food, song, and dance. The Nguzo Saba were so thoroughly instilled into her young consciousness that they became living principles with personalities and demands for attention. Salima resonated most with Kuumba, however, and as an adult, she's relied for the past fifteen years on an ever-replenishing supply of creativity to guide her in using drama and music to share the meaning of Kwanzaa with children.

Salima was part of an ensemble that staged the 1980s hit *What Iza Kwanzaa?* for several seasons at the Afrikan Poetry Theatre in Queens, New York. Later, her presentations at schools, arts institutions, and public celebrations helped to develop a following for a colorful character she created and named "The Kwanzaa Queen." This queen, though regal, never put on airs; she was always festively dressed, ready to have a good time, and able to break the concepts into bite-sized treats that even the littlest members of her audiences could digest.

When she moved to Cleveland, Ohio, ten years ago, Salima brought The Kwanzaa Queen with her, making an appearance in a local production by Black Renaissance in Theater. Her character was instantly loved by children there, which led to the Theater's commissioning of a play, "The Legend of the Nguzo Saba," built around The Kwanzaa Queen. It has since become an annual holiday favorite. Much of Salima's work as an arts educator and consultant involves or is also inspired by Kwanzaa. She's regularly contracted to travel around Cleveland and to nearby counties to provide pre-Kwanzaa workshops and to organize Kwanzaa ceremonies and celebrations.

"This is how I stand," says Salima. "It's what I represent. It's not so much about the holiday for me anymore and I'm not in this for Karenga. It's about what I can do to help, and in this case, it's teaching these principles to our young people as tools for living. The Nguzo Saba is the basis of it all." The Kwanzaa Queen can be contacted at sistasali@aol.com.

Imani

Many would say that "to believe with all our hearts in our people, our parents, our teachers, our leaders, and the righteousness and victory of our struggle" is asking an awful lot. But if any people can pull it off, we can. We have exhibited faith of every category and adjective, from empowering and enlightening faith to the blind and dangerous variety. It's been our compass on countless survival missions, our instrument of choice in many a delicate operation, and our undoing when ill placed. When Black people say, "We've come this far by faith," they couldn't be more serious. But how much farther can it take us? Likely that depends upon the quality of faith we're willing to invest in ourselves, in our people, and in our objectives.

Although faith is by no means peculiar to religion, the subject is most discussed in this context. In the Bible, for example, Hebrews 11:1 says, "Now faith is the substance of things hoped for, the evidence of things not seen." Place emphasis on the "now," because that's what's required; faith you used to have, or plan to have, will not serve you today. Have faith now and have faith in the now. Yes, sometimes it's hard to get to or hold on to. When it is, try adopting a neutral attitude before swinging all the way to disbelief. Refuse to predict doom and gloom for yourself or for your people. It's an energizing habit to keep an open mind that leaves room for beneficial turns of events.

Believing with all our hearts requires a willingness to feel passionately about our parents, teachers, and leaders (many people add "our children" and "ourselves" to the maxim). If you believe that the world is a perilous place for feeling people, remember that those who excel have passion in common, be they ball players or scientists. These people work hard to get to where they'd like to be, often battling self-doubt, physical challenges, and closed doors. They prevail because they believe the struggle is worthwhile and that they will ultimately succeed. Perhaps you find the word "struggle" problematic. If so, consider that Imani doesn't posit that all life should be a struggle, only that struggle is often part of life. Even an infant struggles to take that first breath outside of its familiar water world. But without that first breath, the life awaiting, with its all fascinating facets, cannot be lived.

Spiritual Applications of the Seven Principles

Those seeking to use the Nguzo Saba to enrich and enliven their spiritual practice will be greatly rewarded. There is a wealth of gold to be mined at the core of these Seven Principles. As our ancestors have always claimed spiritual ties to the land, we can view the Nguzo Saba as both vital seeds and essential tools. As seeds they can be sown into the fertile soil of our consciousness; as tools they can be used to measure our growth and reap our harvest. Whatever our faith or spiritual philosophy, the ethical values represented here can help us to look within and to consider the significance of our actions in the world.

The Paris-Cameroon Kwanzaa Connection

Christian Fehem of Cameroon, Central Africa, is one of the founders, along with Ernest and Carol (Coco) Matong, of Association Panafricaine pour la Célébration du Kwanzaa (A.P.C.K.), an organization devoted to popularizing the holiday in Paris, France. Together they've produced seven annual celebrations and the attendance has steadily grown.

"We, the Black community in France—which includes brothers and sisters from Africa, the West Indies, and other parts of the world—need something in common to unify us," says Fehem. "Our organization sees in Kwanzaa a real response to the problems we face in the economic, social, cultural, educational, and spiritual arena." The A.P.C.K. observance includes dialogue, festivities, and a special day, "Le Kwanzaa des Enfants" (The Kwanzaa of Children), for young ones and their families.

"Now family and children know of the event and wait for it each year," says Coco. "They say, 'This is my second Kwanzaa!' or, 'I was here last year, and saw this same girl last year!'"

The Matongs remember being introduced to Kwanzaa by people from the Caribbean living in France. A group was brought together to research the subject and to deliberate together on its suitability to their community and its priorities.

"We were agreeably surprised to discover a thoughtful work, reflective and coherent, which proposed a true alternative to us of which we never had heard spoken in France," Ernest recalls.

Ernest and Coco are booksellers well known to people in the community. They make it a point, year-round, to remain involved and abreast of the issues affecting Black France.

The members of A.P.C.K. enjoy and are committed to their work. On its Web site, the organization says its mission is "to promote the philosophy on which the celebration of Kwanzaa rests so that the Kamit Diaspora keeps long-lived the principal elements of her basic culture."

In 2004, upon the death of his father, Fehem returned home and created KwanzaaCameroon, a leadership training and academic assistance after-school program. Finding it an ideal way to act on and share the values of the Nguzo Saba, he's taught the children, their parents, and their coaches about Kwanzaa.

"I have named my after-school organization 'Kwanzaa,' so I can constantly communicate, by any means necessary," Fehem says. "People always ask me, 'What's Kwanzaa?' 'Where did you get this name and why did you choose it?' This gives me the opportunity to talk about Kwanzaa with them, especially about the Seven Principles, the vision, the philosophy, and how they can live by it. I have to make them know that a tremendous concept deeply rooted in the African culture exists and can help us, wherever we are, to succeed in any way we want."

In addition to its after-school program, KwanzaaCameroon brings parents and students together for a Kwanzaa ceremony and celebration each year. "They're painting and playing roles," says Fehem. "The main objective remains the same: they must memorize Umoja, Kujichagulia, Ujima, Ujamaa, Nia, Kuumba, and Imani—without this, they forget the philosophy of Kwanzaa."

A.P.C.K. can be reached at www.kwanzaa-apck.com. Contact KwanzaaCameroon at fehem@hotmail.com.

Umoja (Unity)

Although we customarily see unity as involving only collective action, fundamental unity begins within ourselves. Are our life's objectives aligned with our highest values? We achieve spiritual unity when we chart a course for the complex of thoughts and energies that compose our inner lives. Having accepted this responsibility, we are able to be more effective in uniting with others around universal spiritual values. Collective meditation, prayer, or group discussion of sacred texts can heighten a devotional experience and lead to action taken to benefit others. Deep contemplation and an expanded awareness of the everyday can lead to the essential realization that all life is one.

Kujichagulia (Self-Determination)

"Defining ourselves" requires paying close attention, muting those voices from within and from without that would have us dishonor our divine birthright and choose a lesser concept of self. We decide what we'll call the divine and what we'll pass on to our children in the way of spiritual concepts. It is our prerogative to define our experiences as individuals and as a people in terms of their impact on our spirit and their significance to our life journey. Exercising our right to self-determination deepens our understanding, helping us to develop into the fully realized people we are meant to be.

Ujima (Collective Work and Responsibility)

Collective work teaches us that although we each have a path to follow, the quest for spiritual enlightenment can also be a communal one. It is often while working on a project to benefit others that we have those "Aha!" moments when a life objective is revealed in a flash. Other people are the mirrors used to show us who we are and the signposts pointing the direction in which we must grow. In working along with others for spiritual or social progress, we learn about reciprocity and the common good. "Response-ability" is the ability to respond in the way we choose rather than merely reacting to an outside impetus. It means no more excuses; neither other people nor situations can make us think or act in any given way. Now we become accountable, individually and collectively, for the things we say and the choices we make.

Haki Madhubuti: Principles Put to Positive Use

Haki Madhubuti was an early champion of Kwanzaa and remains one of its examples of the fruitful returns of living according to the principles. A poet, author, educator, institution builder, and publisher, Madhubuti, along with his wife, Safisha, founded the Institute for Positive Education (IPE) thirty-seven years ago. The Institute's New Concept School for preschoolers, the Betty Shabazz International Charter Elementary School, the Barbara Ann Sizemore Elementary School, and the DuSable Leadership College Preparatory Academy all followed. Together, the four schools currently serve over 1,000 students daily.

In 1967 Madhubuti cofounded Third World Press (TWP), using $400 he'd made reading poetry to purchase a mimeograph machine. Today TWP is a multimillion-dollar enterprise that has published works by the great Gwendolyn Brooks, John Henrik Clarke, Sonia Sanchez, Amiri Baraka, Woodie King Jr., and others. The phenomenal success of its recent publication, *The Covenant with Black America*, is discussed in Chapter 8. Madhubuti's own successful and influential books, including *Black Men: Single, Obsolete, Dangerous?; Tough Notes: A Healing Call for Creating Exceptional Black Men*; and others, have been published through his press as well. He has even penned a Kwanzaa book, and Safisha has written two.

"We started practicing Kwanzaa using the Nguzo Saba as part of our foundation in building values, in 1965," says Madhubuti. "The reason my wife and I have been able to sustain and to establish four schools and the Third World Press is because of our seriousness concerning the necessity of building independent Black institutions. We committed ourselves, inspired by the liberating narratives of the sixties."

Madhubuti feels that reinforcing the values and priorities embodied in the Kwanzaa holiday helps celebrants to move forward purposefully and in greater unity.

"We must not lose sight of the tomorrow we're confronting," he says. "We must study all areas of those things which affect our people" (www.thirdworldpressinc.com).

Ujamaa (Cooperative Economics)

A spiritual approach to Ujamaa suggests that we consider our expenditures from a holistic point of view. An aware person makes an effort to ensure that her time, her energy, and the fruits of her labor are wisely spent. Are we investing our riches, be they mental or material, spiritual or creative, in pursuits that further our goals and progress the objectives of the community? In order to enthusiastically pool our resources with others, we must first feel that we are practicing cooperative economics with persons of like mind. Are we, ourselves, thinking and acting like the enlightened and trustworthy people that we seek? After taking stock of our own development, it takes courage to maintain the open mind and heart necessary for attracting to ourselves the people with whom we can productively work. Once we've assembled cooperative work crews for our various life projects, we must keep the overall mission in the forefront and pay attention to the care and feeding of our relationships. Nurturing that which sustains us and those who support us is Spiritual Culture 101.

Nia (Purpose)

Living on purpose allows us to decide how we'll view and approach life. Why are we here? What contributions can we make? What are our priorities and how do we spend our time? Are our words consistent with our deeds? When we bring our spiritual convictions to the table, our lives have meaning beyond our circle of friends and our area of activity. A purposeful life, one with a mission and a plan that transcends self-interest, glorifies its source. As a people, our spiritual mission has been not merely to survive but to thrive, disproving, in the process, our limitation. As individuals, we are meant to realize our soul's purpose and to discover and develop our talents. As we lay claim to authority over the direction of our own lives, we heal the scars on our souls and honor the sacrifices of Harriet Tubman, Frederick Douglass, and others whose spirits demanded nothing less than courageous conviction.

The Kwanzaa Collective

Twenty years ago in New York City, a couple of Kwanzaa stalwarts became concerned about the commercialization of the holiday and decided to unite as an opposing alternative. Michael Hooper, founder of Roots Revisited, approached Mzee Moyo, head of the International African Arts Festival, and suggested that the groups collaborate and bring in others to help preserve Kwanzaa's traditional spirit and grassroots applications.

"Kwanzaa had begun to lose its cultural significance in the community," says Hooper. "The East at one time offered seven days of Kwanzaa in an armory, a number of the freedom schools observed individually and collectively, and there were Kwanzaa ceremonies going on everywhere in people's homes back then. I said, 'We need to bring this thing home to Central Brooklyn and build on it.'"

The Kwanzaa Collective's composition of member organizations has varied over the years, but the two founding groups, along with the Committee to Honor Black Heroes, have been consistent. The initial format was for each organization to take one of the seven days and be responsible for programming and financing it. "Over the years the Kwanzaa Collective has brought many organizations and individuals together for meaningful celebration," says Moyo. "There is always high-energy African dancing and drumming, sometimes jazz, drama, and children's presentations. The member groups cosponsor it, so admission is free and we feed everyone. We also give the 'Keepers of the Flame Award' each year to people who've kept the principles alive in their work in the areas of the arts and culture, education, and economy."

If you're traveling to New York City around Kwanzaa time and would like to join The Kwanzaa Collective in celebration, call (718) 638-6700 for information.

Mama Kuumba

Ella Coard, or "Mama Kuumba" as she was widely known, was for decades, before her passing in 2004, the embodiment of the Kwanzaa spirit in Brooklyn, New York. Mama Kuumba's students at Uhuru Sasa and Black Genius on the Rise learned a great deal about their heritage and they carried their pride along with them long after leaving school. Many of these young people, who honed their knowledge of Kwanzaa under her tutelage, grew up to celebrate with their own children.

Mama Kuumba could be counted on to come to the rescue in any Kwanzaa dilemma; if something needed for the table was unexpectedly misplaced, no one would worry if Mama Kuumba was invited. Most likely she'd have the item in the big bag she always carried with her to a celebration: the one bulging with books, games, and other zawadi for the children, African-print wrapping paper, statuettes, gourds, banners, benderas, posters, and more. She knew the Nguzo Saba backward and forward and all the Kwanzaa songs and was always the most enthusiastic celebrant in the room over the age of six.

Taiwo Coard remembers that his mother not only revered Kwanzaa, but lived its principles each day. Their apartment was filled with miles of books, and young people from the neighborhood could come by and use them to learn their history. Coard says he saw lives change as a result of that access. His mother took the name "Kuumba," one of the Nguzo Saba, because she resolved to make creativity her tool of choice in serving her community.

Coard and his sisters and brothers had no choice but to represent Kwanzaa. He says they were taken to hear Karenga speak each year, they had the Nguzo Saba meanings memorized, and they often performed with the Weusi Kuumba Troupe during Kwanzaa week.

"My mother wanted to spark within people the energy of Kwanzaa, which, to her, was fertility," says Coard. "That's how she saw the concept of 'first fruits.' She also understood the spirit of Kwanzaa, and there was no commercialism in her bones. She did it because she loved it."

Kuumba (Creativity)

A spiritual approach to Ujamaa is informed by the acceptance of our oneness with the Creator. It embraces the premise that to be human is to be granted an inheritance of infinite creativity. However, we are expected to learn to use our tools wisely, as thought is powerful and word is productive. Our people have always been supremely creative, making a way where there was none and pulling resources from the proverbial hat. Much of the great art we've contributed, be it visual, literary, performance, or other, has been prompted by our need to reflect the beauty of our spirits despite our circumstances. We named our music "soul," after its source. Our spiritual challenge is to be conscious creators, seeking to honor the divine within ourselves and inspiring others to seek their highest expression as well.

Imani (Faith)

Keeping the faith is critical; without it the mission fails. Faith is a master's instrument, not a fool's game, as the "things not seen" are often the crux of the matter. Dictionaries define faith as "belief, despite evidence to the contrary." But remaining faithful is less challenging if the evidence we seek is the "not seen." We believed in our people when we were unseen and unheard, when even our humanity was denied. Faith was, and is, an indispensable survival tool. It's imperative, therefore, that we maintain the right to choose our own belief systems without relying on outside approval. But as frequently as our faith is put to the test, how often is it put to the task? What are the uses of faith? Can it move mountains, shift paradigms, lower blood pressure, or send illness into remission? Many scientists and theologians concur that it can. So we are wise to keep faith in ourselves, in the benevolence of the universe, and in our right to insist on a better world.

Chapter Three

Preparing an Authentic Celebration

SUCCESSFUL Kwanzaa gatherings are joyful and inspiring. Whether you're planning a simple observance at home, playing host to friends, or helping to organize a public event, a meaningful Kwanzaa celebration requires a little planning, particularly for first-time celebrants. Those new to Kwanzaa should first make certain they have an understanding of its basic principles; Kwanzaa veterans will find this review of the principles inspiring, as well. Readers can look for additional material on Kwanzaa, particularly that written by Dr. Karenga. (See Chapter 9, "Kwanzaa Resources.")

Reflection on the Nguzo Saba allows participants to bring something significant to the family table each evening and to the gatherings they will host or attend. Consider, as you go about your day, if you've promoted collective work and responsibility on the job (Ujima), helped to maintain unity in your family (Umoja), or patronized a small business in need of your support (Ujamaa). Consciously reflecting on the Seven Principles can result in a richly satisfying ceremony.

It's helpful for families or groups to become familiar with the components of the Kwanzaa ceremony and to decide who will fill which roles. (A detailed description of the key aspects of a ceremony is provided in Chapter 4.) An attempt should be made to include everyone who's interested in taking part, if not in the ceremony itself, then in the planning. Commitment and reliability are more important than experience in this case, as working collectively should ensure that information and support are available.

Consider if visiting friends or relatives would be pleased to play a role in the ceremony. If you think so, contact them beforehand to find out what they might like to do. They can choose a historical passage to read, light a candle, make a favorite dish, or bring a small artifact from home to be placed on the Kwanzaa table.

Whether it's your first or thirtieth Kwanzaa, a little strategic planning helps things to run smoothly. Some points to consider: Will the person presiding pour the libation and lead the songs or will someone else? Will this person light the candles, invite various individuals to do it, or supervise children in the lighting?

Take time to identify additional ways in which everyone can actively take part, especially if yours will be a family observance. Perhaps an elder can contribute a legendary dish or make the first phone call to family members, inviting them to attend. At the ceremony, this elder or another could recall a historical event or share an incident in the family's past that illustrates the application of one of the Nguzo Saba.

Determine at which point in the ceremony you'll invite participation, such as in the presenting of an anecdote or perspective relating to a principle. Some ceremonies start out this way and the candles are lit in conclusion, while other Kwanzaa celebrants prefer to complete the ceremonial steps, followed by discussion and reflection.

If both you and your fellow celebrants are new to Kwanzaa, select someone to lead the ceremony and make certain he or she will devote some time to becoming familiar with the symbols, language, and procedures. Consider dividing the duties between two people if necessary, or assigning aspects of the ceremony to some of those who plan to attend. Seven people can be chosen, for example, to each memorize the meaning of one of the Nguzo Saba. Or one person can be prepared to speak on the importance of ancestral tradition, while another addresses the role of elders and children in the community.

A Kwanzaa ceremony and feast can leave a lasting impression on those in attendance, providing nourishing food for thought in the year ahead. So have fun while planning and acknowledge your part in creating something enlightening and inspiring. Among longtime observers you'll find those who fast for a short period prior to these seven days; others will fast from sunrise to sunset throughout the week of Kwanzaa. The fast is intended to cleanse the body, discipline the mind, and uplift the spirit. Some persons who are called on regularly to preside at Kwanzaa ceremonies will prepare by spending a little time in quiet reflection beforehand.

If you'll be presiding, think about the type of experience you'd like to create for those who'll gather to celebrate. The objective for a family ceremony may simply be an enlightening good time in one another's company, or it could involve deepening the family's convictions regarding one of the Seven Principles. An agency or member organization might like to use the event as an opportunity to raise awareness and rededicate people resources. Will you lead a ceremony in which everyone makes an action-oriented commitment to addressing an issue, a ceremony characterized by laughter that eases the process of honest self-assessment, or one that combines both? Your focus and approach help to set the tone.

Choosing a Date and Inviting Guests

If you live in an area where Kwanzaa is widely celebrated, you know there can be many a karamu (celebration) to choose from on Imani, the final day. In some communities, several celebrations may be held on each of the seven days. You'll want to first determine your priorities—what would you like to have done by the time the Kwanzaa week comes to a close? If your focus is family, do the candle-lighting together in your household as often as possible during the week. Then to schedule the karamu, take a poll of other family members and choose a date that's convenient for most.

If you're planning a karamu to which friends and business or organization colleagues will be invited, you might do a little local research to determine which dates are not as heavily scheduled. Or resolve to host the karamu on whichever day holds significance for you or your group and cheerfully celebrate with those who are able to attend. Also consider your venue: If the public is invited, it should be wheelchair-accessible and not far from public transportation if some guests will arrive that way. Planning a large gathering can be a bit overwhelming. Consider hiring the services of a local event planner if you don't have the time or the help you need to prepare for your karamu while meeting your other responsibilities.

As Kwanzaa gatherings are most often informal, there's usually no need to order printed invitations. Your guests will, however, enjoy receiving one of the many festive packaged invitations that you can buy at Black bookstores or shops selling cultural gifts. If the time or inclination is lacking, an invitation via telephone or e-mail is usually fine. Evite™ and some other free online services allow you to check periodically on who has received your invitation and whether or not they plan to come. Your invited guests can leave messages for you at the site and you can send updates or request that someone bring a dish or an item you'll need. You also have the option of allowing them to add other guests to your list.

A word about etiquette for online inviting—use the features considerately. Some of your guests will not want everyone on your list to view their e-mail address, for example. Also avoid, if possible, sending invitations to someone's workplace, and offer guests the option of replying via your personal e-mail address or by phone. If you're on the receiving end of the invitation, remember that everyone may be able to view your response, so choose your words with care and don't click on "maybe" unless you'll most likely attend. You may be seeking a polite way to say you're not coming, but the host will be spared needless preparation time and expense if you're honest. Try to say "yes" or "no" early on, and if you won't be attending, thank the host for considering you and ask to be invited again (assuming you mean it).

Of course, nothing works quite like a phone call. A printed or online message can tell someone that you look forward to seeing them, but in speaking with you, they can hear and feel it. Oftentimes you'll find friends who might have declined due to the fatigue of managing jobs or family will reconsider when they hear your voice; they may realize they miss you and look forward to being energized in festive holiday company.

Involve the Children in the Planning

Children love Kwanzaa and can be involved in a number of ways. First, talk with them about it, explaining why and how the family (or the class, or the group) will celebrate. Tell them about the origins of the holiday and its importance, and where it's celebrated across the world. Use language and examples they can comprehend: knowing that a parent will return at the end of the school day is an expression of faith (Imani); completing a homework assignment demonstrates purpose (Nia); Harriet Tubman's commitment to the Underground Railroad was Kujichagulia (self-determination) in action.

If your children have observed Kwanzaa before, praise them for what they remember. If this will be their first time—look out! Kids like anything new and they love holidays, so expect them to be super-excited. Learning about Kwanzaa can be a welcome addition to your child's routine year-round, with the focus intensifying as the holiday approaches. Then together, you can review a principle a day for seven days, memorizing its definition while picking up toys or food shopping. Talk to them about historical figures and people in their own family lineage who have exemplified one or more of the Nguzo Saba. Discuss the meaning of the various symbols and the order of the ceremony over dinner and sing Kwanzaa songs while giving the children a bath.

Retired New Jersey kindergarten teacher Jwajiku Korantéma, author of the children's book *I'm African and Proud,* devised several fun ways to teach her students about Kwanzaa and has found incorporating music and dance to be significant.

"I made up a Kwanzaa song for the children, usually a new one each year," says Korantéma, "and then we'd put on some music and create a dance together in which each principle has its own movement. Educators know that movement is a tool for cognitive learning; the body stores the memory, so that each time the children perform a specific movement, they remember that principle."

Help them to feel a part of the preparations from the beginning by working with you to create a list of guests to be invited. Children who are not writing as yet can call out the names of family members and friends to be listed. If you'll be mailing invitations, children can, according to their age and abilities, help to pick out Kwanzaa cards, address envelopes, or paste on stamps. Allow your child to take part in deciding on a cultural outfit to wear; if there are none in her wardrobe, no problem. Shopping for traditional African attire or for the fabric to make a garment can be both fun and educational. Now let your child help to select music for the karamu as well as any games to be played, and you have a bona fide Kwanzaa-ready kid. Your only concern may be a case of intense calendar watching.

Menu planning is always a favorite with kids. Do a little research together to come up with a few traditional African recipes and discuss traditional African-American dishes. Then ask them to help you to create a menu that has some of each, including one of their own favorites or Grandma's special dish. Plan the food-shopping trip along with them; they can help make the shopping list and help put the items in the cart or basket. Identify ahead of time how children can help with the cooking and discuss kitchen safety. They'll anticipate helping out and will know what to expect as well as what's expected of them.

Ask the children for ideas about decorating their home or classroom to beautifully reflect the spirit of Kwanzaa. Have a few suggestions of your own ready as well. They can draw or paint pictures depicting Kwanzaa themes and symbols such as the Mishumaa Saba (seven candles). Other subjects can include a Kwanzaa gathering, Black heroes, or family ancestors. Perhaps they can make an African mask to hang on a wall or mold a Kikombe cha Umoja (unity cup) of clay and paint it in bright colors and a traditional pattern. Musical instruments that shake and rattle are quick and easy to make. They're a fun addition to the karamu (feast), along with bells strung to be worn around the wrists or ankles while dancing.

Children can also create all kinds of things to give as Kwanzaa gifts (zawadi). They can cut out pictures of people of African descent around the world from old issues of *National Geographic* and pictures of important figures in Black history from back issues of *Ebony* and *Jet*. These can be used to make a collage poster or to decorate the cover of a journal. With a little help, younger children can make hand puppets and cloth dolls and accompany you to the store to help select art supplies for their young friends and relatives.

Necklaces, bracelets, and ankle bracelets are fun to make, and a trip to the bead store is always a hit. Belts, picture frames, and hair ornaments can be made using cowry shells. This project can be accompanied by a brief history of how these shells, which children see everywhere today, were used in traditional Africa. Teenagers can make a CD compiling traditional African music from the family's collection or from the Internet. They can also pick out books for siblings and younger children who'll be attending the celebration.

These are a small number of the many ways in which parents and teachers can engage children prior to and during Kwanzaa. See Chapter 9, "Kwanzaa Resources," for a listing of a few Black history games, arts and craft books, stores, and more.

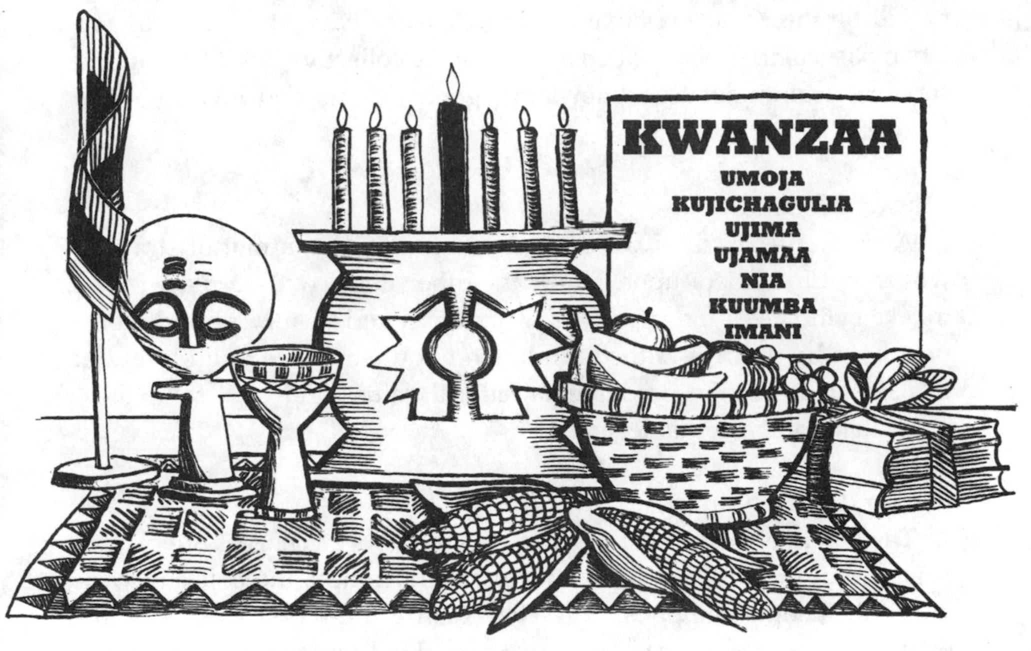

A Beautiful and Traditional Kwanzaa Table

There are seven symbolic items placed on the Kwanzaa table and two supplemental items to be displayed on a nearby wall. They are:

Mazao (Crops)

Mazao are the crops—they are what yields from an investment of time and energy spent cultivating soil and planting seeds. As most people of African descent no longer grow their own food, the significance of the mazao surpasses the physical. Fresh fruit and vegetables are placed on the Kwanzaa table to symbolize the harvest or the fruits of labor, particularly the productive outcome of collective labor. The mazao serve as a reminder to acknowledge good fortune and joyfully share the wealth.

Mkeka (Mat)

At the center of the Kwanzaa table is the mkeka, a mat of straw or woven natural fibers upon which the other items will be placed. The mkeka symbolizes the support that tradition and history provide for a people's way of life and the foundation upon which we build a future. It also stands for the fundamental ethical values and cultural expressions that compose this legacy.

Kinara (Candleholder)

The kinara is the candleholder in which the seven candles are placed. It is a focal point of the festive table and references the collective origin of the people: the physical forebears, ancestral roots, and the motherland, Africa. The descendants are many, held together by a common means of support. Kinaras are traditionally carved from wood and inscribed with symbols of our heritage, but they can also be made of metal or clay.

Muhindi (Corn)—Also Called Vibunzi

Ears of corn are placed on the Kwanzaa table in recognition of the blessing that is children and the future that they represent. Just as one ear has many kernels, one person can produce a long line of descendants, who can, in turn, produce still more, safeguarding the people's future. Customarily, one ear of corn is placed on the mkeka for each child in the house. If there are no children living there, then one or two ears of corn can be placed to symbolize children who have matured and moved out, the potential or desire for children, or for those who have no children, the acknowledgment of shared responsibility for the community's young ones.

Mishumaa Saba (Seven Candles)

The mishumaa saba represent the Seven Principles and the seven days of Kwanzaa. They are placed in the kinara and lit, one each day, until all are burning on the final day. There is one black candle, three red, and three green. Black symbolizes the people. Life comes through us and happens to us; it is the people who must take action that will result in progress. Red stands for struggle, the exertion required to make this progress. It honors the sacrifices of the ancestors to ensure the survival of their descendants and is a reminder of the work still to be done. Green signifies the land of Africa, the prospects for the future, and the fruits of conscientious labor.

The black candle is placed in the middle, with the red candles to the left and the green to the right. On Umoja, the first day, we light the black candle for the unity of Black people. It is lit again on the second day, Kujichagulia, along with the red candle adjacent to it. On the third day, Ujima, we light the previous two and the green candle flanking the black one. On the fourth day, after the three previous candles are lit, we return to the left side to light the red Ujamaa candle third from the center. This pattern follows until all the candles are ablaze on the day of Imani.

Kikombe Cha Umoja (Unity Cup)

The kikombe cha umoja is one of the primary symbols placed on the mkeka. It is preferably a hand-crafted cup, most often made of wood or ceramics, and represents the foundational unity that must be nurtured in order for a people to achieve the fullness of their potential. The cup is used to pour a libation to the ancestors and to salute the prospects of the people.

The two supplemental symbols of Kwanzaa are not placed on the table, but displayed prominently and in close proximity, usually on a nearby wall. They are the following:

Bendera (Flag)

The red, black, and green striped Pan African flag was conceived in 1920 by Marcus Mosiah Garvey, founder of the Universal Negro Improvement Association. Originally, the red symbolized the bloodline uniting people of African ancestry; black represented the people and their history; and green was for the fertility of the African homeland. In recent years, Dr. Karenga has reinterpreted the order and significance of the colors to be: black for the people, red for their struggle, and green for the better future resulting from that struggle.

Nguzo Saba Poster

This lists the Seven Principles for all to see. It serves as a reminder of Kwanzaa's foundational objectives to those who have assembled. The poster is usually a decorative one produced and distributed by marketers of African cultural products. However, a homemade poster, perhaps made by or with children, can also be displayed as an inspiring embodiment of Kuumba.

As you plan to secure the seven primary and two supplemental items for a Kwanzaa ceremony, give some thought to how you might like to personalize and beautify your Kwanzaa table. A length of African print fabric is used as a tablecloth on which the mkeka and other items are placed. Some people add a sculpted or drawn ankh, which is the ancient Kemetic icon for "life." Others include West African Adinkra symbols, particularly Sankofa, the bird with its head turned backward, signifying: "Go back and fetch it" (reconnect with your past).

A small drum can be placed on the table to represent communication among the people and connection with the ancestors. On many Kwanzaa tables you'll find a bust, small figurine, or other African artifact denoting the genius and breadth of the African arts. A photo of an indigenous African person in traditional dress can signify common cultural heritage. The plant that will receive the libation can also be placed on the table, representing nature, continuing growth and vitality, and the promise of the future.

Kwanzaa Greetings and Other Terms

Take some time in the weeks leading up to Kwanzaa to learn the Kiswahili words integral to the holiday. Review them several times a week with family and friends, particularly if you'll be a host. Mastering even a few of the terms will make a difference; you'll feel better connected to the ceremony and more confident about leading or participating at a gathering. If you have children around, you have a built-in advantage—involve them in learning the terms and they'll make sure you get lots of practice!

Habari gani? (Ha-ba-ree GAH-nee) "What's the news?" or "What's happening?" It's the traditional greeting to open a Kwanzaa ceremony and when encountering someone in person or answering the phone on each of the seven days. The reply is the principle represented that day, so the exchange would proceed: "Habari gani?" "Umoja!" (Question: What's happening? Answer: Unity!), and the greetings follow suit for the remaining six days.

Karibu (Kah-REE-boo) "Welcome."

Tafadhali (Tah-fah-THA-lee) "Please."

Asante (Ah-SAHN-tay) "Thank you."

Wimbo (WIM-boh) "Song." A Kwanzaa ceremony should include at least one Kwanzaa song.

Tambiko (Tam-BEE-ko) "Libation," which is poured.

Tamshi (TAM-shee) "Statement," as in opening or closing words.

Harambee! (Hah-rahm-BAY) "All pull together!"

Tutaonana (Too-ta-oh-NAH-nah) "Until we see one another again." This is customarily said when departing.

Create a Vibrant Kwanzaa Setting

If you'll be observing Kwanzaa at home, you can energize the space by decorating up to a week in advance and your preparation can highlight the personal touch. You likely own several items that can be used to reflect heritage, beauty, and creativity. Begin by looking around your home or apartment to get decorating ideas. Perhaps pull out that special piece of African fabric you seldom use and see how it would look draped over a mantle, sofa, or doorway. A strip of cloth (make sure to trim or hem the edges) can accent a window treatment.

Plan to use color to help create a festive environment and feel free to mix patterns and hues in an attractive manner. This is completely in keeping with traditional African style. Kente cloth, a woven fabric made in Ghana, West Africa, is often used to lend a regal, special-occasion look. Its rich earth tones mixed with purple, bright blue, red, gold, and green can serve as a color theme around which to design. Plan also to incorporate the red, black, and green color combination; its significance is explained earlier in this chapter.

Paintings, sketches, and coffee-table books that depict historical or cultural scenes can be showcased. Certainly if there are children in the home who have produced art reflecting their heritage, it should be on display. Healthy plants, handmade crafts, and functional items made of natural materials, such as straw baskets and wooden bowls, can also be featured prominently. If you have traditional African drums and other hand-played instruments in your home, make sure they're brought out to be seen and heard during the ceremony and karamu.

Look for places to showcase any African sculpture you might have, or plan to buy an inexpensive piece. Kwanzaa does not promote consumerism and you can likely decorate your home without having to make purchases. However, if you've been planning to spruce up a bit, this can be a great opportunity to explore the wide range of culturally inspired home furnishings and accents created and sold by community artisans. Along with sculpture, batik, and mud-cloth fabric, you can purchase beautifully carved stools and picture frames, African-print throw pillows and lampshades, hand-painted vases and switch-plate covers, and many other items.

Keep these ideas in mind also if you're part of the planning team for a larger event, as many of the same elements will apply. Appoint someone with a talent for design to serve as head of the decorating committee. If the group plans to rent a space, have the committee visit beforehand to assess what's needed. Four bare walls can often be transformed into a beautiful and lively environment with a little TLC.

To keep decorating costs low, each committee member can bring African cloth, a painting, an artifact, and a plant from home. Likely there will be some people eager to contribute multiple items for the evening, making the task easier. Use affordable solid-colored fabric as tablecloths if you can, or see if the venue you're renting provides them. If you end up with white, however, look for colorful runners or festive disposable placemats.

Start early to identify providers of the items you'll need to celebrate Kwanzaa and comparison-shop. Make sure that, in the spirit of Kwanzaa, you begin with local merchants. Don't be concerned if there are not many shops such as these to choose from where you live; there are lots of small businesses outside your area that carry the items you need. Many of them ship orders via the Internet, so take a little time to browse for those things not available to you locally. (See Chapter 9.)

Zawadi: Meaningful Gift-Giving

The exchanging of zawadi, when done in the spirit of Kwanzaa, should be stress-free and enriching for both the giver and the receiver. The focus is never on trends, price tags, or appearances, so feel free to show your appreciation for others in a creative and affordable manner. Many people accustomed to a high-pressure holiday season have found this a liberating experience. The message it sends to young people—that of content over commerce—is an added bonus. Kwanzaa gifts are traditionally educational, cultural, artistic, or a combination of these. In the decades since its inception, celebrants have come up with many innovative gift ideas in keeping with the holiday's objectives.

As with the other aspects of Kwanzaa preparation, it helps to have a plan. If you'll exchange zawadi at a gathering of family or friends, discuss beforehand what will work best for everyone. Keep in mind that the giving of zawadi is not the primary focus of the holiday or of the gathering. It should be done in the spirit of Maat, the Kemetic (ancient Egyptian) principle, which upholds as one of its tenets, "Giving, seeking nothing in return." If it's made clear at the outset that gifts do not necessarily have to be reciprocated, givers will not feel slighted nor recipients obligated.

Some families give zawadi only to the children, but most people delight in gift giving, so it's perfectly acceptable for other adults to be on the receiving end. There are also longtime and new Kwanzaa celebrants who observe a handmade-gift-only rule. A flexible approach is usually most successful, however, as not everyone has the skill to create a handmade gift or the time to learn how. If opting to allow each person to do as they choose, your family or group commits to honoring the thought behind each gift. This means Aunt Clara should cherish your imperfect handmade gift as much as the new book someone else gave to her. (Find how-to craft books and websites in Chapter 9, "Kwanzaa Resources.")

There is a wide range of things from which to choose when considering zawadi for the Kwanzaa table, including books and other learning tools, great music, enlightening DVDs, wearable art accessories, and Black art or history wall calendars, as well as shea butter, essential oils, and other natural products. Whatever you choose, honor the spirit of Ujamaa by making every attempt to purchase your gifts from Black-owned businesses.

Books are probably the most commonly exchanged gift during Kwanzaa time. In purchasing them, consider your objective. If you're seeking to inspire someone to express their writing talent, for example, books on the craft will help, as well as poetry chapbooks or anthologies, classic novels, and new fiction. Books on art, music, dancing, photography, film, design, and other endeavors can also aid in the creativity campaign.

Of course, the inspiration factor particularly applies when selecting gifts for children. A budding photographer will be fascinated by a Gordon Parks bio written for children or a set of postcards featuring James Van Der Zee's work. A young artist might love a book that includes a photo of "The Harp," by gifted sculptor Augusta Savage, or painter Elizabeth Catlett's "Sharecropper." The book *Gifted Hands* by Dr. Benjamin Carson, the first neurosurgeon to successfully separate twins connected at the head, might help a teen decide on medicine as a mission.

The story of Ruby Bridges, who, in 1960, became the first African-American child to desegregate an elementary school, models courage during challenging times. Teens will enjoy reading about the stand taken by boxing great Muhammad Ali and about Olympic great Abebe Bikila of Ethiopia, who ran a 26-mile marathon barefoot. One story that never fails to capture the minds of children is that of Harriet Tubman. She exemplified Kujichagulia as the uncompromising "general" who led slaves to freedom on the Underground Railroad.

For teens, consider Hil Harper's *Letters to a Young Brother*, Anna Deveare Smith's *Letters to a Young Artist*, or Terrie Williams's *Stay Strong: Simple Life Lessons for Teens*. Engaging and challenging reads for young adults interested in hip hop culture are Bakari Kitwana's *The Hip Hop Generation: Young Blacks and the Crisis in African American Culture*, Tricia Rose's *Black Noise: Rap Music and Black Culture in Contemporary America*, or Joan Morgan's *When Chickenheads Come Home to Roost*.

To provide resources for expanding an adult's or teen's knowledge of their heritage, give books on history and culture and consider biographies, folklore, and collections of proverbs along with scholarly texts. Include books written by historians and independent thinkers of African descent, including Carter G. Woodson, Cheik Anta Diop, Franz Fanon, Harold Cruse, Ivan Van Sertima, Chancellor Williams, Yosef ben Jochannan, John Henrik Clarke, Amos Wilson, Maulana Karenga, Tony Martin, Herb Boyd, Robin DG Kelly, Amiri Baraka, Molefi Asante, Randall Robinson, Angela Y. Davis, Marta Vega, Ra Un Nefer Amen, Joy Leary, Muata Ashby, bell hooks, James Baldwin, and Wahneema Lubiano. This is, of course, an abbreviated listing—a little research will reveal many more choices to make and voices to be heard.

Some of these texts are considered among the Great Black Books. Of course, you'll find several opinions on which titles compose this list, but certain books will appear consistently. Louis Young is founder of the African Heritage Academy (AHA!), a developing institution promoting mastery of African intellectual heritage. Interestingly, his top ten titles, most of which are books, include two works of fiction:

1. *The Husia*
2. The Odu Ifa (the wisdom of the Yoruba)
3. *Narrative of the Life of Frederick Douglass*
4. David Walker's Appeal (an antislavery document)
5. *The Souls of Black Folk*
6. *Up from Slavery*
7. *Philosophy and Opinions of Marcus Garvey*
8. *The Collected Works of Langston Hughes*
9. *The Fire Next Time*
10. *Invisible Man*

Many fiction titles are rich in history, and others offer profound insights through contemporary tales. A gift of fiction can sometimes create new, or newly enthusiastic, readers of those friends and family members who rarely indulge. Good fiction has been known to change lives. Often readers who don't respond to essays or to advice-laden books will see themselves in a character. They may also see strategies and hope. Think of the novels or short story collections you've enjoyed and those that made a lasting impact; consider which of them would be appropriate for which friend. Give responsibly, keeping the spirit of Kwanzaa in mind. The storylines should be inspiring, modeling ethics and courage, emotional healing and growth.

Some authors to consider include: Toni Morrison, John Oliver Killens, Ralph Ellison, Zora Neale Hurston, Octavia Butler, Alice Walker, Walter Mosley, John Edgar Wideman, Henry Dumas, Toni Cade Bambara, Maryse Conde, Edwidge Danticat, Randall Keenan, Colson Whitehead, Gloria Naylor, Alice Randall, Reginald McKnight, Marita Golden, and many others.

Great poetry makes a fabulous zawadi as well. Choose from collections that include the work of Langston Hughes, Gwendolyn Brooks, Margaret Walker Alexander, Sonia Sanchez, Haki Madhubuti, Elizabeth Alexander, June Jordan, Welton Smith, Jayne Cortez, Robert Hayden, Ed Spriggs, Mari Evans, Yusef Komunyaaka, Amiri and Amina Baraka, Nikki Giovanni, Raymond Patterson, E. Ethelbert Miller, The Last Poets, Carolyn Rodgers, Audre Lorde, Dudley Randall, and Lorenzo Thomas. More recent anthologies may include Safiya Henderson Holmes, Sekou Sundiata, Tom Dent, Jessica Care Moore, Darryl Holmes, Willie Perdomo, Jacqueline Johnson, Saul Williams, Sharrif Simmons, Kevin Young, Staceyann Chin, and Tracie Morris.

There are, of course, many things other than books to give as Kwanzaa gifts. In looking to Africa for inspiration, choices can include small artifacts or other inexpensive decorating items, African-themed pottery, posters or prints, and items made of African fabric, including dashiki shirts, hats, infant outfits, throws, and napkins. A small musical instrument such as a cow bell or Kalimba (thumb piano), a recipe book, a hairstyle guide, or Oware game will likely be appreciated. A child will love a doll dressed in traditional garb or an African-themed coloring book or puzzle. In the United States many people of African descent have some Native American ancestry as well, so books on the various nations or craft items made by their people are also in line with the heritage-honoring spirit of Kwanzaa.

Other gift ideas include a ticket to a Black film festival screening, museum exhibition, or show; a prepaid dance class, yoga class, or nutritional consultation; family photo CDs; or a scrapbook. Consider also a subscription to a Black magazine, a gift certificate to a local Black bookstore or boutique, a charitable donation or a contribution to a public radio station in the recipient's name, or a Black history trivia game. Some unique gifts are inexpensive and even free. You can visit a currency exchange and trade a few dollars for beautifully illustrated African paper money. Or in the spirit of Ujima, offer service—perhaps giving a single dad a handmade certificate he can redeem for a home-cooked Sunday dinner for his family.

Looking as Good as We Feel: Traditional African Attire

The wearing of traditional African attire at Kwanzaa ceremonies has meaning beyond the superficial. Adorning yourself in the patterns, color combinations, and garments created by your ancestors honors their cultural legacy. It recognizes the vast contribution made by African peoples to the wearable arts, the establishing of an aesthetic that has influenced style throughout the world. When you join with others in dressing in traditional attire, you strike a common chord and create a galvanizing link through time, connecting you to both your forebears and the next generation. You also honor those who struggled for basic rights such as the ability to demonstrate pride in one's heritage.

In choosing traditional clothing, you're making a conscious statement, not wearing a costume. Although gatherings are most often informal, there is a Kwanzaa ceremony performed, so African attire can, in this context, be viewed as ceremonial dress. If you can remain in ceremonial mode through the seven days, that's wonderful and powerful; if not, consider wearing cultural jewelry or another accessory that reminds you you're celebrating Kwanzaa. Be flexible about dress if you're lighting the mishumaa saba at home with family each evening—the willing participation of family members and the discussion of the day's principle are more important. When planning for a karamu, however, create an environment enhanced by cultural attire. While guests who arrive in jeans or more formal Western attire should never be made to feel uncomfortable, it is your prerogative as host to request traditional wear.

When inviting your guests, whether by phone, e-mail, or snail mail, simply say: "African attire, please." Don't be concerned that you'll scare away friends and relatives; you're simply stating your preference as the person who's extended them an invitation. They'll know that you'd like them to make an effort to comply, but few will take it as seriously as they do "black tie only." Those new acquaintances or friends-of-friends who can't pull together an outfit in time will usually come anyway, with or without an explanation.

Of course, there are many people who wear traditional African or African-inspired clothing on a regular basis. They can be a source of information on locating garments or fabric to make some on your own.

There are also Black clothing designers of all ages who incorporate African themes in their work, offering a number of current or forward-looking outfits suitable for Kwanzaa celebrations. These designs may feature the flowing lines of many traditional African garments, be accented by patterned trimmings, or enhanced by cowries or beads. There are many sources of African outfits for adults and children. See Chapter 9 for a few suggestions, ask for local recommendations in your area, or browse the Web.

Harambee!
LET'S ALL PULL TOGETHER!

Chapter Four
THE KWANZAA CEREMONY

THE Kwanzaa ceremony enlivens the Seven Principles, serving as an inspiring vehicle for discussion of higher values and rededication to common objectives. In this chapter we'll explain how to set up the traditional Kwanzaa table, which is the focal point of the ceremony. Also addressed is what happens during the ceremony, the order in which the candles are lit, their correspondences to the Seven Principles, and other information you need to help things run smoothly. While this chapter prepares you to conduct a meaningful ceremony, tips for hosting a successful karamu (the feast, or party that often follows a ceremony) are shared in the next chapter. Also, there are a few Kwanzaa books that contain sample programs to use when planning a public event.

A Kwanzaa ceremony can be as straightforward or as structured as you like, depending on your preference and time. It will, however, always include a few fundamentals, whether you're celebrating in your household or in an auditorium. First you'll need to follow the simple steps to setting up the Kwanzaa table; at home it will remain in place throughout the seven days. Choose one large enough to accommodate your plans for adorning it. If you're at home and have little space, you may want to use only those items that hold symbolic meaning in the ceremony. On the other hand, don't let the fact that your ceremony will be home-based stop you from doing more if that's what you'd like. If yours is a public ceremony in a large venue, use some of the decorating suggestions provided previously to create a festive cultural ambiance prior to setting up the table.

The first step in setting up the Kwanzaa table is to cover it with decorative African fabric. This can be print, kente, indigo, mudcloth, or another of the traditional textiles. Next, place the mkeka in the middle of the table with the kinara centered on top. Position the mishumaa saba within the kinara and bring your mazao to the table in a large, decorative wooden or ceramic bowl. If you'd like your table to reflect overflowing abundance, arrange additional fruits and veggies around the base of the bowl or in a few clusters around the table.

The muhindi are next and, if there are more than one, are grouped together on one side of the table. Your kikombe cha umoja is then positioned prominently, usually to the front and side of the kinara. Make sure that the bendera is displayed nearby, facing the east, and that the Nguzo Saba poster is behind, above, or adjacent to the Kwanzaa table. Finally, have fun using the decorative items you've selected to make your Kwanzaa table uniquely your own. (See Chapter 3 for a full explanation of the Kwanzaa table items and their symbolic meaning.)

Some public ceremonies have been known to feature elaborate and beautiful Kwanzaa tables. Forces of Nature Dance Theater in New York City, for example, is known for creating a huge Kwanzaa table that looks like a mini–produce market. People who attend their celebration leave laden with cantaloupes, apples, grapes, cabbages, cauliflower, and, of course, lots of corn.

Let's Celebrate! Opening the Kwanzaa Ceremony

At the start of a basic Kwanzaa ceremony, the presiding person extends a greeting and welcome on behalf of the host. Then this person obtains clearance from the elders present, a traditional African gesture of respect. The ceremony leader will turn to the oldest person in the room and ask permission to proceed. If it's not clear who the oldest person might be (looks can be deceiving), the leader can ask, or address the elders as a group. This permission is always given immediately. If, however, you're presented with the rare exception of an elder who's reluctant to grant permission, he or she is probably enjoying the attention and seeking to prolong it. Ask if the elder would like to say a few words to the group first—that should do it.

If the ceremony is a household one, the family member who is presiding can make a brief statement reflecting the significance of what is about to take place. At a larger gathering this will be done by the ceremony leader. This is a good time to review the meanings of the symbols, particularly for those present who are celebrating their first Kwanzaa. The ceremony leader should go briefly over the items on the table and also talk about the significance of the bendera's colors. Encourage everyone to participate, particularly the children. Those little ones who know the names or meanings will be excited to show what they've learned.

Now a libation is poured in honor of the ancestors, either by the ceremony leader or someone previously identified to fulfill this role. This person will use the kikombe cha umoja to pour a little water into a plant while calling out the names of those who have gone before, either in the direct family line or persons who had furthered the aims of the group. Then come those who are thought of as guardian spirits and heroes, with the people assembled calling out names.

In a family setting the person pouring might say, for example: "*We remember you, Grandma Marie, for teaching us life lessons with humor, and you, Aunt Joyce, for bringing the family together for holiday meals. We salute you, Grandpa James, for your example of leadership in building the family business. We thank you, Frederick Douglass and Rosa Parks, for standing up for our rights . . .*"

At a larger or public gathering, the person pouring libation will not usually call family names, but will mention those revered by the community. These will be both historical figures and people who had worked alongside those assembled. It might resemble this: "*We honor those in our families who worked hard so that we could thrive, and those ancestors whose names we do not know. We are thankful to those who struggled for our freedom, some sacrificing their lives. We salute you, Harriet Tubman; you, Marcus Garvey; you, Denmark Vesey; you, Touissaint L'Overture; and you, Yusef Iman.*"

Upon the calling of each name (or category of persons), a little water is poured. When signaled, people will call out any additional names they'd like to include, be they family members, unsung heroes, icons of the arts, organizers and political activists, inventors, healers, historians and other educators, clergy, or humanitarians. While these names are called in unison across the room, the last of the water is poured in small portions. The libation draws to a close with a statement appropriate to your ceremony, such as a traditional African salutation or a simple giving of thanks. If there is something else planned in honor of the ancestors, perhaps a song or poem, it should be done at this time. Limit this to one or two things, however. ("The Bridge of Honor," a poem for the ancestors, is included at the end of this chapter.)

An original Kwanzaa custom is for the kikombe cha umoja to be passed around for all to take a drink as a symbol of unity in practice. Following the libation, or later, before the Harambee, the ceremony leader would take the first sip and then the cup would be passed around until each person present had sipped. It is still done this way at many public gatherings and particularly in family households.

In the last two decades, however, some celebrants have altered this practice when at larger gatherings. Not wanting to drink from the cup after strangers, they substituted alternate gestures. One is to distribute paper cups to everyone and fill them from the unity cup. Then everyone drinks in unison, much like a toast, with the ceremony leader sipping from the kikombe cha umoja. If you find yourself at a ceremony in which the unity cup is circulated and you don't want to sip, but also don't wish to offend, hold the cup up to your lips and make a sipping gesture, smile, and pass it on. Likely, the only ones who'll notice you didn't drink are those people sitting very close to you. Your relaxed smile should help them to accept your gesture in the Umoja spirit you intended.

Reasoning and Singing Together

The ceremony leader now turns to those assembled and asks, "Habari gani?" ("What's the news?") In answer, the group calls out in unison the name of that day's principle, for example, "Kujichagulia!" (Self-determination!) The ceremony leader can recite the maxim given by Dr. Karenga or give someone else in attendance the opportunity to recite it. A discussion of the principle then proceeds, optimally with participation by all present. This is often the most memorable aspect of the ceremony, as insights, anecdotes, and sometimes feelings are shared. It can deepen the significance of a principle for everyone, leaving something to chew on long after those take-home plates are finished. If you're a guest at someone else's Kwanzaa ceremony, try to contribute a few words if asked; your participation does help.

If someone has prepared a song, short folktale, a harvest dance they've learned, or a poem addressing the day's principle, it should be shared at this time. If a speaker knowledgeable on Kwanzaa or a related issue has been hired for a public ceremony, that person should make their presentation at this time. If not, move right into the Kwanzaa wimbo (songs). These are not done performance-style, but sung together by everyone present. Some Kwanzaa songs are call-and-response, some mention the Seven Principles and others do not, but they are all fairly brief and simple to learn. (Chapter 7 contains Kwanzaa songs and a Kwanzaa rap.)

Make the singing of the wimbo a joyous experience. If you're doing the ceremony at home, ask people to clap to help keep time; if you've invited several guests or are having a large gathering, have a drummer on hand. While people can sit and sing if they like, dancing is always welcome. It works best to have a song leader who knows the songs and whose enthusiasm is infectious. If this person is also the ceremony leader, fine. This person should review each song first, reciting it slowly without music or other accompaniment, so that those hearing it for the first time will grasp all the words and feel more comfortable.

Lighting the Kwanzaa Candles

Now that the wimbo have been sung and the room is infused with Kwanzaa spirit, everyone gathers around the Kwanzaa table for the lighting of the mishumaa saba. The seven Kwanzaa candles are lit in a certain order: The black candle is lit for Umoja, then the red one directly to its left for Kujichagulia, then for Ujima, light the green candle directly to the right of the black one. This continues, alternating between the red and green candles adjacent to those already lit. If you are observing along with your household, the family gathers briefly each evening to light the candles. The black candle only is lit on the first day, with the others following in the order above on each subsequent day. So on Day 2, you will light the black candle and the first red one. On Day 3, you will light these two again and the first green one, and so on, until all seven are lit on the final day. As each of the mishumaa saba is lit, the principle associated with it is named and its meaning recited.

It's a good idea once again to involve the children as much as possible, whether at home or at a larger ceremony. They love to light the mishumaa saba and take great pride in it. In fact, most children pay closer attention throughout the ceremony when they know it will culminate in them playing such a significant role. Of course, the ceremony leader must stand right there to strike the match for those who don't know how, and to grasp the hand holding it for little ones or those wary of the flame.

Often at public Kwanzaa celebrations, all seven of the mishumaa are lit for the purpose of discussion and to commemorate Kwanzaa as a whole. At other large ceremonies, however, the only candles lit are those that correspond to the present day and those that have passed. Either way you choose to do it, there will likely be more children present than there are candles to light. If so, ask for volunteers by a show of hands in the air and choose objectively from among these. If the host's children would like to light a candle, it's a nice gesture to choose one of them. Most likely they've been helping their parents get ready for this day and they're super excited.

Obviously, the ceremony leader shouldn't choose only little kids or only girls, and there are ways to allow additional children to play a role. For example, as one child lights a candle, another can announce the name of its principle and share a little about it. The ceremony leader should also say a few words about each principle following the lighting of its candle and, if time permits, solicit a few comments from among those gathered regarding how they see and act on that principle.

A word about the mishumaa saba: Make certain that they are safely used. If the table is in the center of the room, for example, and there will be little children running around, you may want to move the kinara to a high mantle or put the candles out after the ceremony.

Testimony and Harambee!

After the candles are lit, those gathered are invited to speak about something they've accomplished over the year and to publicly rededicate themselves for the year ahead, perhaps declaring a new goal. They can also commend others present who have made accomplishments, particularly the children and young adults. At this time the ceremony leader can select someone to speak on behalf of all assembled, giving thanks to the Creator for the bounty of the harvest—the growth and blessings that the closing year has brought.

When the testimonies are complete, everyone who is able rises to their feet for Harambee (Hah-RAHM-bay), which means "all pull together." Harambee is done by raising the right arm high above the head, palm open and fingers spread, then pulling it down energetically, the hand closing into a fist on the way down, and ending with the arm bent and held close alongside the torso. This symbolizes the unifying of the people: moving from separation to cohesion, from the singularity of fingers to the powerful strength of the fist.

The ceremony leader or someone with a rousing voice stands before the group and says the following (or substitute a Harambee preamble of your own making): "Now it's time for us to join in Harambee! Let's all pull together! We're going to pull down seven loud 'Harambees!' for the family, community, nation, and race; for those who have passed on and for those yet to come. And we'll hold the last one until we run out of breath! On the count of ja, li, tu!—Harambee, Harambee, Harambee, Harambee, Harambee, Harambee, Harambeeeeeeeeeeeeeeeeeeeeeeeeeeeeeeee!" (Don't forget that the "ee" sounds like "ay.")

Undoubtedly, you'll have a few people who ham it up, making a pretend show of holding the longest breath. This usually results in the children collapsing in a fit of giggles, which is a great way to end a Kwanzaa ceremony. The distributing of the zawadi, discussed in Chapter 5, follows directly after, usually while the food is being served (buffet style is fine). Enjoy, and make memories.

The following is the poem mentioned above:

THE BRIDGE OF HONOR

(For the ancestors)

We call across the waters
bridging space and time to reach you
those who are never far
from our hearts
from our minds
Our call is breath rippling the lake
stirring memory

invading the stillness
mining the depths

Our hearts beat in these breaths
These breaths sound through the waters
These waters are life itself
Life itself is inspired by us
We make our impression upon life
that much deeper and more lasting
by partnering with you

How much easier
how sweet the flow
When we know
we are supported
encouraged
valued and heard
We feel honor in your regard
We regard you with honor
Back and forth
across this divide
that is a filament of light
we travel
in the light
our hearts uplifted
We travel light

We speak your names
and are empowered
by your ever-presence

intimate and epic
Your gifts of legacy
evoke pride in our past
Your gifts of vision
serve to open our present
Your gifts of love
help ensure our future

We call across the street
to reach you
recognizing you in one another
reaching out our hands each to the other
walking, talking, vessels of ancestral inspiration
We honor what we see
We honor what we do not see
We fear not
We trust
We must
Across the bridge of honor
we travel
in the light
blessedly gifted
We travel light

—Maitefa Angaza

Chapter Five

A Festive Kwanzaa Karamu

THE karamu (feast) is the social gathering that often follows a ceremony and is one of the most anticipated aspects of a Kwanzaa celebration. It's a time for laughter, good food, and catching up with the news in the company of loved ones and colleagues, old friends and new. Breaking bread together helps to reinforce the notion of a collective harvest as well as our commitment to support one another. Sharing our talents promotes free expression and builds trust, just as making music and dancing together reveal the joy in building community.

Imani, the final day of Kwanzaa, is the traditionally designated feast day, but a karamu can, and will, be scheduled at any time during the week. If Kwanzaa is not widely celebrated where you live, the karamu you'll likely attend will be a family or extended family event. If the holiday is also new to your family, be prepared to do the hosting or organizing. If your family members are Kwanzaa veterans, however, you'll have an easier time delegating and collaborating.

As a karamu usually requires planning, shopping, and cooking, many families will gather just once, often on Imani, the final day. Sometimes, however, two or more family members will want to host a karamu at their homes. Add invitations from friends along with public events organized by local groups and institutions, and you can have one busy season! If this is what Kwanzaa is like where you live, you know it helps to plan which celebrations you'll attend. Most likely you'll be asked to bring a dish to one or more of these gatherings, so have your favorite recipes on hand or test-run a few new ones.

Distributing the Zawadi

Zawadi time should be brief and festive. As host, you can set the tone by highlighting the care that goes into the selecting of zawadi and the privilege it is to receive them. When the gifts are handmade items, books, cultural products, and wearable art, the environment is not usually fraught with tension, frantic with euphoria, or weighted with disappointment. There are lots of smiles, however, along with excitement and appreciation. Children see that books are prized articles, that adults can take time to create something with their own hands, and that people will be genuinely touched by simple gestures. Some guests will want to see and know about another's book or artifact, so there's often informative dialogue as well.

Elders attending the karamu should be first to receive their gifts. This signals the respect they are due according to African tradition and models for the youth a willingness to honor that respect. While the elders are opening their zawadi, have someone distribute the children's gifts. If the karamu is a family gathering, the zawadi may be tagged as intended for specific children. For a more public gathering, however, the host can estimate the number of children who'll be attending and direct guests to bring one or two small items to be given to any children of a particular age.

If you're using an online invitation, you might attach a message to it saying, "We need six zawadi for boys aged nine to twelve, four for toddlers," etc. Have your guests commit online to bringing one or two items from your list, so everyone will know what's covered and what's still needed. Some guests will opt to bring more and reply: "I have four puzzles for children aged six to ten," or, "I'm bringing three beaded bracelets for teen girls." Place a few extra requests on the list to cover children who show up unexpectedly. Many times a family or two that you've invited will bring a cousin who's in town for the holidays or a friend who's spending the night. The giving and receiving of zawadi should be drama-free, and it's asking a lot of a young child to be the only one in the room without a gift.

If someone present has given or received a promise of service as a zawadi, make sure that the children are present to witness it. This helps reinforce for them the nonmaterial focus of Kwanzaa and demonstrates that giving of oneself is highly valued in the community.

Menu Planning for the Feast

A Kwanzaa karamu will have an abundance of delicious things to eat—it's not called a "feast" for nothing! If you're part of a group hosting a public celebration, establish a food committee to share the work of planning a menu, doing the shopping, preparing the food, and setting up a serving area and system. The objective is to make sure that things run smoothly, that everyone has enough to eat, and that guests enjoy several of their favorite dishes. Plan a menu that includes some of the staple foods eaten by people of the African Diaspora. In the United States, for example, this will include traditional Southern dishes such as greens, black-eyed peas, and sweet potato pie. In the Caribbean, a host may serve peas and rice, plantain, callaloo with okra, root vegetables such as dasheen, as well as dishes made with curry or coconut.

This is also an ideal time to serve traditional African dishes, becoming acquainted with them if they are unfamiliar to you and your guests. West African favorites such as jollof rice, tiébou dienn, and groundnut stew and Central African dishes such as zom, ugali, and futari will add authentic flavor to your celebration while adding to your culinary vocabulary. There are lots of cookbooks, old and new, as well as Internet sites to use as resources. Some culinary sites feature chat rooms in which members swap recipes. There may be someone who has made the dish you're interested in or who can offer suggestions and encouragement. Consider other resources as well. You may have a friend who is a whiz at new recipes or who has more time to experiment. If there is an African restaurant where you live, you can ask them to recommend a dish that will likely be a hit and order enough of it to add to your menu.

No matter what type of food you'll be serving, it's helpful to shop early for the necessary ingredients. If you're making a new dish with spices hard to find in your area, allow time to order them online or from a catalogue. Stock up on the more conventional (and nonperishable) ingredients and start planning your meal. Be honest with yourself about what you can successfully manage, asking family members to pitch in and scratching a few dishes off your wish list if needed.

Do you want guests to contribute by bringing a dish or dessert? If so, who's known for making a particular dish better than anyone else? Put your request in early. Which dishes need prep time and which are better made a few hours before? Are you inviting guests who have food allergies or dietary restrictions? Do you need to borrow a punch bowl, extra serving dishes, or utensils? Consider if you'll need additional plates, and if they'll be ceramic or higher-quality paper. Also have extra plates and foil wrap on hand; at the close of the gathering you may have extra food you'll want guests to take home. If you're planning on using glasses, you'll want to have paper cups for the kids. Think about where will people eat and if you have enough chairs. Fortunately a karamu is almost always an informal gathering, so pillows on the floor will work just fine for some of your guests.

After all your hard work, make sure you give some thought to preservation and presentation. If you won't have room to store all the food that needs refrigeration, make arrangements with a friend or neighbor. One or two friends can be assigned to bring ice cream if you'll be serving it and another can bring bags of ice and buckets to keep the ice cream and your beverages cold. Some foods can be prepared early and frozen, but not all dishes retain their appeal after thawing; be sure you know which is which. Think about ways to keep everything looking and tasting fresh. Know which foods may change color when wrapped in foil and when to use lemon to slow oxidation.

How will you present the food to your guests? Bread served in a basket lined with festive cloth is immediately more appetizing, and fresh parsley used as a garnish will enliven a platter of fish. A border of cherry tomatoes brightens a plate of veggies, and the proper mix of colors makes a salad irresistible. Decide early what cloth you'll use to dress the table, and look around for napkins and other items in complementing colors. Beautify the food table with a centerpiece of fresh flowers, a lush green plant, or an arresting figurine.

Music Makes the Day

Music is an integral part of a memorable karamu, so if you're hosting, make sure your gathering will sound and feel good. Live music is always a treat in keeping with African tradition, as is communal dancing. Invite your musician friends to jam at an acoustic set and have the dancers open the floor, encouraging others to join them. Have at least one good drummer there to establish rhythms that can be built upon by a shekere, cow bells, flutes, a marimba, berimbau, or other instruments.

Yusef Waliyaya—The Kwanzaa Griot

Making Kwanzaa accessible fun for young people was a mission for the late Yusef Waliyaya, poet, playwright, musician, and composer from Brooklyn, New York. A cofounder of the Queens-based Afrikan Poetry Theatre, Waliyaya used its stage to educate about African history and culture, often through storytelling punctuated by his playing of rhythms on the drums and on flute. He had a particular gift for wedding music to poetry in a way that captivated children, and his band, The Medicine Man YaYa and The Black Cross Nurses, eased adult audiences into an Afro-funk groove.

His passion for the meaning and spirit of the holiday made Waliyaya an irrepressible information source as Kwanzaa approached each year. He was billed as "The Kwanzaa Griot," for many of his presentations for children, and he wrote and produced the play *What Iza Kwanzaa?*—which introduced the holiday's concepts enveloped in music and spectacle. Its intended audience of little folk adored it and the play ran for years at Waliyaya's home theater and also toured schools and community centers across New York City.

"I performed with Yusef as one of his Black Cross Nurses," says his sister, Donna Coulter. "I remember his love for Kwanzaa and that he was always on the go at that time of year. Our family saw firsthand his love for Black people and his drive to teach African history through entertainment. He wrote to the end."

Three of Waliyaya's Kwanzaa songs are included in this book, and his CD, *Teach the Children: A Tribute to African American History in Song and Poetry*, is available new and used on amazon.com.

Let the neighbors know there'll be drumming and dancing. They may not mind, but will appreciate your consideration. If the prospect of bearing with the music and other festive sounds is unattractive to them, they can plan to be away for a few hours. Either way, your prior notice will lessen the probability of neighbors showing up at your door to ask that the music be silenced.

It's fun to have additional instruments such as tambourines and harmonicas on hand, so guests can join in the music-making for a while. Limit this to a certain period, however, in order to make room for both freestyle fun and quality entertainment. If you've hired a group to play, you'll, of course, want to feature them, so ask them at which point guests should participate. Usually this works best toward the end of a set, rather than at the beginning; once your guests get started making music, they may not want to stop! The professional group may also be able to provide background music for the karamu, depending on how long they'll be around.

If your live music will be provided by musician friends you've invited, keep in mind that they are first and foremost your guests. They'll enjoy a little uninterrupted time to play with peers skilled in tempo and improvisation. And if the musicians are having fun—everybody's having fun! Your musicians can expend lots of energy playing and will get thirsty, so keep water or another beverage nearby. Have someone set plates of food aside for them before the most popular dishes are gone, and make sure they take time to eat and socialize. Your musician friends will also have good suggestions of recorded music to play.

It's best to have some CD selections identified and located early. The right choices will help your family or guests to enjoy a wonderful karamu, whether or not you have live music. Traditional African drumming, Afrobeat, and jazz are among the preferred options, as well as those R&B and reggae songs with a consciously positive message. A Kwanzaa CD is an obvious choice, and there are various types available. While all are festive, some combine good music with empowering Kwanzaa-related lyrics, and others focus on including music from across the African Diaspora, which may be instrumental or sung in other languages. There are also Kwanzaa CDs made for children, some using rhyme and character voices to help young ones grasp and remember basic Kwanzaa themes. Chapter 9, "Kwanzaa Resources," points readers to several sources of music suitable for a Kwanzaa karamu.

Dancing in Celebration

Traditional dance of the African Diaspora can add a vital dimension to a karamu. Whether the dancers are members of a professional ensemble or guests drawn to the dance floor by the pull of the rhythms, the energy they generate can be invigorating for everyone gathered. If your family or organization can hire a dance troupe to perform at your

karamu, it will almost certainly be a wise investment. Of course, if you're not familiar with the dancers in your area, you'll want to get recommendations or plan ahead of time to see a few groups in performance.

If you think you would like to hire a troupe, find one that will perform in traditional costume and whose members or spokesperson can explain to your guests the origin and significance of the dances they'll perform. Many traditional African groups will have dances of welcome and celebration as part of their repertoire, along with salutes to the ancestors and Mother Nature. Some will even know and perform a harvest dance. If funds and/or timing do not permit the hiring of a troupe, consider a single dancer. A good traditional dancer accompanied by experienced musicians can enliven your karamu and uplift your guests, particularly if he or she can coax them onto the dance floor.

Professional dancers are an option, but by no means a necessity. Guests at a karamu can entertain themselves by dancing together in celebration. A good drummer or a great CD can get the first few people up to dance, and they'll inspire others to join them. If you're usually the first one on the floor, you can plan to get the dancing started at your karamu. Or if neither you nor your friends are likely to break the ice, identify at least one guest who will. Approach that person ahead of time and enlist their help. Once the dancing is under way, it should take care of itself, as long as the music remains right. Pretty soon the high spirits and mix of personalities will make for an infectious good time.

For a warm and joyous karamu, set an inclusive tone and safeguard it. Pull aside anyone who begins to judge or make fun of another's style of dance. Remind them that in gathering to celebrate Kwanzaa, we re-create the African village, where community is fostered through acceptance of individuality. People of all ages and body types should feel free to express themselves in movement. Often a crowd-pleasing elder will want to show that he or she's still got the moves. Teens should be allowed to do the latest dance, as long as it's appropriate. Young children love to dance with parents or older siblings, so allow them to do so for a while, and then guide them to an adjacent area to dance with one another. Some adults feel hampered in their movements when young children are underfoot and others are not sufficiently aware in their movements. Designating a bit of space for the little ones will prevent them from being hurt and allow them to dance with their customary energy and abandon.

An Opportunity to Share Our Talents

Along with the good food, music, and company a karamu offers, Kwanzaa celebrants also look forward to the pleasure of a soulful song, a powerful poem, and the sharing of various other expressions of talent. There's usually a supply of developing—and often hidden—talent in the room at any given karamu. If yours is a gathering that will last "until . . . ," you can freely ask if anyone present would like to share. Or if you need to adhere to a schedule, try factoring in some Kuumba Time. The result may well be a delightful addition to the festivities, such as a bit of dance, or dialogue from a scene in a play.

Encourage each person to be considerately brief (maybe cap it at five minutes) and to present something in harmony with the values and objectives of Kwanzaa. Be flexible with the little kids; some may want to display their mastery of the alphabet, a talent for making faces, or a new knock-knock joke. Older children should be asked to share something meaningful; if they're reciting rap lyrics, these should have a productive, respectful, and profanity-free message. Best would be lyrics they've written themselves.

Of course, an effort can be made to call the young people together before the karamu to help them to prepare something to present. The younger children will require one or more adults to plan the presentation, but should also be allowed to contribute their ideas. Older children may want to work together on a skit or on individual presentations with a little supervision. They should be encouraged to use their Kuumba to come up with something entertaining and educational and given the freedom to use humor when appropriate.

Storytelling is often a hit at Kwanzaa time and can be a captivating way to pass on history and cultural values. A good storyteller can add vitality and depth to a karamu, offering something that all generations can enjoy together in the African tradition. The right person will have a collection of proverbs and tales memorized and will be able to convey the drama, wit, and wisdom they offer. You may be surprised to learn that someone you know is an accomplished storyteller; you'll never know until you ask around. If there isn't anyone coming to your karamu who can tell a good tale, consider hiring someone. Storytellers usually work for reasonable fees. They love what they do and their enthusiasm is infectious. Look for information on contacting them in Chapter 9, "Kwanzaa Resources."

Some friends and relatives may want to share information rather than talent. A guest may ask to read a piece of writing they've done or share something else that they feel suits the occasion. This may be perfectly fine, depending upon your preferences and the nature of your karamu. The optimal scenario is for the host to be informed beforehand, but that's not always the case.

While some people view the karamu solely as a vehicle for relaxed and pleasurable social interaction, others see an opportunity to reinforce community objectives. An activist karamu can be an electrifying experience and a powerful way to look forward to the year ahead. If that's what you'd like to take part in creating, go for it! Invite passionate people who will relish this type of gathering and sit back and enjoy. If, on the other hand, you'd prefer a lighter mixture of dialogue, entertainment, music, and dancing, you'll have to make that clear at the outset and be prepared to steer your karamu back on track if a guest takes the reins.

Similarly, you'll want to be on the lookout for anyone who tries to use your karamu as a platform from which to promote their business, sell products, or solicit donations for an organization without your permission. The karamu can, in keeping with Ujamaa, be an ideal place to let others know about a product or service. But if this is not done in the right manner, your guests will feel uncomfortable, or worse, used, and the festive energy can dissipate. You don't want someone breaking into conversations or following other guests around in an attempt to push an agenda or a product.

If you'd like your karamu to serve as a place for guests to exchange this type of information, establish a time period in which this will take place, and stick to it. Perhaps the ceremony leader can introduce business owners, inspiring everyone to celebrate their success and to support them. If you'd rather keep the focus more on the celebration and the Kwanzaa principles, set up a table where guests can leave and take business cards, flyers, and brochures.

Think about some of the other things you enjoy and consider making them a part of your karamu. It could include the showing of a culturally relevant and inspiring film not usually seen in most venues. If you'd like to include an independent film at your karamu, browse the listings of Third World Newsreel at www.twn.org to rent or purchase one on DVD or VHS. Your karamu might be an occasion for young and old to be creative together. Shrim Sa, a Brooklyn-based spiritual organization, hosts a Kwanzaa ceremony and karamu each year that allows everyone to contribute to the making of a collage. Paints, pastels, glue, and magazine photos are kept in view so guests, including the children, can use images to express their thoughts on the principle for that day.

Fun and Games at the Karamu

Game nights are popular among some who've celebrated Kwanzaa for many years. They know that the focus will be clearly on the Nguzo Saba during the ceremony and discussion, and they opt for fun and games afterward. A game night can be combined with entertainment and social dancing if a time period is set for each, or if games are played in an adjacent area while the karamu proceeds. Black history trivia and board games are fun. Try Journey to the Motherland™, Blackboard™, or others. Charades with Black–themed clues are good for adults to play along with children aged ten or older. Everybody can join in a game of Oware, Uno™, Go Fish!, or Pictionary™.

Have children's games on hand for the younger kids, particularly games that involve singing, moving around, or building basic skills. Remember that little kids want to play anything that looks like fun, so decide beforehand if you'll partially or completely accommodate them. Who Am I?™ and I Can Do Anything™ are positive board games for little ones. Some six-year-olds play a decent game of chess or checkers and may ask to join in for Scrabble™, Taboo™, or blackjack. You won't be playing for money (no, you won't!) and you may not mind them participating, but consider that those guests who've anticipated some serious game-playing might mind.

If you do play games, your karamu may be a lengthy one; keep in mind that tired, wired, or weepy little ones can add stress to the festivities. Setting aside a room or area where children can play noisy games or lie down later on can help to make happier campers of everyone. The children don't have to suppress their abundant energy, and their parents and the other adults can enjoy some time together. Just make certain that someone is designated, on a rotating basis, to check in on or be with them, particularly if the children are very young or in an unfamiliar environment.

A word about teens: While the discussion of the Nguzo Saba and the karamu entertainment are clearly important for everyone to share, teens should also be encouraged, but not required, to join in the game playing. Even though they often end up having the most fun at the game table, they may prefer to spend some of this time with one another. Try to compromise on this, as you'll want them to feel that there's a place for them to socialize at the karamu as well. Teens shouldn't, however, be allowed to seclude themselves for the duration, even if they're accustomed to doing so. Remind them that in keeping with the principles of Kwanzaa, they should share the wealth that is their company with others.

Last, but surely not least, make sure that *you* have fun. Even if you enjoy hosting so much you're usually inclined to overdo it, resist that temptation. At Kwanzaa time you'll want to make sure that you're upholding the principles as best you can. Sometimes that means accepting help. Some of those people who'll ask, "What can I do to help?" really do want to help. To insist that they sit by while you run yourself into the ground is not in the communal Kwanzaa spirit, so share the wealth and enjoy your celebration!

Chapter Six

RECIPES FOR THE FEAST

MAIN DISHES AND SIDES FROM NEAR AND FAR

Baba Mzee's Stuffed Blue Fish

Fish

8 pounds blue fish, filleted
a pinch of fresh thyme
a little sliced ginger
a little fresh garlic
a pinch each of curry, cayenne, and Cajun seasoning

Rub cleaned fish with fresh lemon. Combine the remaining ingredients, and rub the mixture inside the fish. Marinate for 24 hours in the refrigerator.

Stuffing

chopped green and red sweet peppers
chopped onions
a little sage
a pinch of cayenne

Sauté together and stuff in marinated fish. Bake at 400 degrees until tender, no more than one hour. Serves 5.

Jennie's Sweet and Sour Chicken

(Courtesy of Tamika Chatman)

2 packets Lipton's Onion Soup Mix
1 cup brown sugar
4 tablespoons spicy mustard (or more to taste)
1 bottle barbecue sauce
16 ounces peach preserves
8 chicken legs
8 chicken wings

Make the onion soup with boiling water, as directed. Add the sugar, mustard, barbecue sauce, and preserves. Mix well. Arrange the chicken in a large saucepan and cover with the sauce mixture, setting a little sauce aside. Cook on medium flame until tender. Remove from heat and brush with the remaining sauce mixture.

Coconut Biscuits

2 cups flour
2 tablespoons sugar
1 tablespoon baking powder
1 tsp salt
½ cup butter or margarine
1 cup milk
2 tablespoons creamed coconut
1 cup sweetened flaked coconut, toasted

Preheat oven to 450 degrees. Combine the first four ingredients in a large bowl. Cut in the butter until the mixture is pea-sized. Add the remaining ingredients and stir until dough is formed. Drop onto a cookie sheet to make 15 biscuits. Bake for 10 minutes or until golden. Serve while still warm.

Cameroon: Zom (Spinach with Meat)

2 pounds stew beef, cut into small cubes
4 tablespoons oil
1 large onion, chopped
2 pounds spinach, washed and chopped
2 tomatoes, chopped finely
1 tablespoon tomato paste
2 tablespoons peanut butter
salt and pepper

Put the beef in a saucepan with a little salt and enough water to cover. Bring to a boil, covered, and simmer for 1½ to 2 hours until the meat is just tender. (It will cook more later on in the recipe.) The time will vary depending on the cut of meat and the size of the pieces. Remove the meat and keep the liquid.

Using a large pan, heat the oil and soften the onion. Add the meat pieces and cook for two minutes.

Take 2 cups of the reserved beef broth. Add water if necessary, then pour this in the pan with the onion and meat. Add spinach, tomatoes, tomato paste, peanut butter, salt, and pepper. Bring to a boil and then cover, reduce heat, and simmer for 30 minutes, stirring regularly. Serve with rice. Serves 6 to 8.

West Africa: Groundnut Stew

- 1 or 2 sweet potatoes peeled and cut into cubes
- 1 or 2 chickens, cut into large bite-sized pieces, or equal parts chicken and beef
- peanut or safflower oil
- salt (to taste)
- black pepper (to taste)
- water or chicken broth (optional)
- 2 or 3 tomatoes, chopped
- 1 or 2 onions, chopped very fine
- 1 clove garlic, minced (optional)
- 1 or 2 hot chili peppers, chopped (optional)
- ½ teaspoon teaspoon ground ginger or coriander
- a pinch of thyme or a bay leaf
- ¼ cup dried shrimp or dried prawns (optional)
- 1 sweet green pepper chopped (optional)
- 1 squash, chopped (optional)
- 1 medium eggplant or a dozen okra, or canned beans, or canned corn (optional)
- 1 cup roasted unsweetened peanut butter

Boil or steam sweet potatoes until tender. In a large pot or dutch oven, fry the meat in hot oil until browned. Add salt and pepper. Reduce heat, add a cup of water or chicken broth, and simmer. Heat oil in a skillet. Fry the tomatoes, onions, garlic, and chili peppers over high heat. Add spices. Add the optional vegetables, sweet potatoes or yams, and/or dried shrimp or prawns. Reduce heat and stir in peanut butter and a bit of water or broth. Stir until smooth. Add the tomato-onion-peanut mixture to the simmering meat. Stir thoroughly and continue to simmer until the meat is cooked and the vegetables are tender. Serve with rice.

Senegal: Tiébou Dienn Fish with Red Rice

1 cup loosely packed cilantro leaves
4 scallions (white and green parts), trimmed and cut in large pieces
3 cloves garlic, peeled
1 teaspoon crushed red pepper flakes or 1 Scotch bonnet pepper, stemmed, seeded, and minced
2 pounds firm-fleshed fish fillets, such as tuna, shark, or swordfish, cut into 1-inch pieces
2 tablespoons palm oil
7 to 9 tablespoons canola oil
5 cups water
4 teaspoons salt (or more to taste)
1-inch piece any type dried fish (optional)

Choose 3 or 4 of the following vegetables:
1 medium cassava (about 1 pound), trimmed, peeled, and cut in 2-inch pieces
1 large orange yam, peeled and cut in 2-inch pieces
1 small eggplant, unpeeled, cut in 2-inch pieces
4 large carrots, peeled, and cut in 1-inch pieces
6 large or 12 small okra pods, stems removed
medium cabbage (about 3 pounds), cored and cut in 2-inch pieces
2 tablespoons tomato paste
2 cups long-grain white rice
12 preserved tamarind pods or 12 quarter-inch pieces of seedless preserved tamarind (optional)
soy sauce or Maggi Liquid Seasoning as a condiment (optional)

Finely chop cilantro, scallions, garlic, and half the pepper in a blender. Add 1 tablespoon of the canola oil and process until smooth. Slice horizontally through center of each piece of fish, leaving one side attached. Fill opening with about 1 teaspoon of cilantro mixture. In a large pot, heat the palm oil with the canola oil, until nearly smoking. Add fish cubes, being careful to keep the filling inside. Cook until done on all sides but still raw in the middle, about 3 minutes per batch. Remove from pot and set aside. Pour off all but 1 tablespoon oil. Add water, 3 teaspoons salt and dried fish, if using. Bring to a boil. Reduce to a simmer. Add longer-cooking vegetables to the broth first, then shorter-cooking vegetables. Simmer, uncovered, until tender. Cassava will take about 50 minutes; yam about 35 minutes; eggplant and carrots about 20 minutes; okra about 12 minutes; cabbage about 8 minutes.

Remove cooked vegetables to a bowl with a slotted spoon. Season with salt. Add fish to the broth. Simmer until cooked through, about 3 minutes. Remove to a plate with a slotted spoon. Season with salt. Measure the cooking liquid. Return it to the pot and add enough water to make 5 cups. Whisk in tomato paste and remaining crushed or red pepper. Stir in rice. Bring to a boil. Reduce to a simmer. Cover and cook for 20 minutes. Uncover and place tamarind pieces, if using, over rice. Cover and cook for 2 minutes. Discard dried fish, if used. Fluff rice with a fork. Place on a large serving platter, mounding it in the center. Place fish and vegetable pieces evenly over the top of the rice. Serve immediately.

Caribbean Rice and Peas

1½ cups dried red kidney beans, soaked overnight
1 clove garlic, crushed
salt to taste
½ cup unsweetened coconut milk
2 scallions, chopped

2 sprigs fresh thyme
1 whole Scotch bonnet pepper or habanero chili
black pepper to taste
salt to taste
2 cups long-grain white rice or brown rice

Boil the beans with garlic and salt until tender. Save 3 cups of the liquid, discarding the garlic. Return beans and liquid to pot (add water if needed) along with the coconut milk, scallions, thyme, chili, and black pepper and salt to taste. When it comes to a boil, add the rice and boil for 20 minutes. Remove from the heat and let it sit for 15 minutes. Stir lightly with a fork before serving.

DESSERTS DONE RIGHT FOR THE KARAMU

Mignon's Yummy Deep Dish Apple Pie with Apple Gravy

Filling

6–7 medium-sized apples of your choice (Mixing gala, Macs, red and golden delicious, Rome, and Granny Smith can be nice.)
⅓ cup brown sugar
⅓ cup white sugar (or fructose sugar)
3 teaspoons cinnamon
½ teaspoon ground allspice
¼ teaspoon ground cloves
juice of ½ lemon

Apple Gravy

4 tablespoons butter

3 tablespoons all-purpose flour

1 cup apple juice or apple cider

½ cup brown sugar

Crust

2 frozen deep-dish pie crusts (one for the bottom and one for the top)

Preheat oven to 350 degrees. Peel and slice apples and place in a large mixing bowl. Coat apples with sugars, spices, and lemon juice. Mix thoroughly with a spoon or fork. Set aside. In a medium saucepan on a medium flame, melt butter. When butter is completely melted, gradually add flour, one tablespoon at a time, stirring vigorously after each to avoid lumping. Let brown slightly, then very slowly add apple juice, stirring constantly until a smooth gravy forms. Add sugar and stir until well mixed. Turn off flame and let cool for about 15 minutes.

While gravy cools, prepare bottom pie crust as per package directions. Carefully add apple mixture to bottom crust, arranging so that there is a peak in the center (a mountain of apples). Pour gravy over the apples, being careful not to let gravy overflow. For the top crust, let second frozen crust defrost slightly (about 5 minutes) so it is soft enough (not too soft!) to mold. Gently remove from tin and cover the apples. Make sure to center it directly on top, allowing the edge to meet with the bottom crust edge. Use fork to go around edge, gently mashing the two edges together. Make 4 steam holes by pricking the top crust gently with a fork. Place pie in the center of a baking sheet and bake for 45 minutes to an hour. The baking dish will catch the bubbling liquid. Let cool for 30 minutes or more.

Optional: Combine 2–3 tablespoons of melted butter and a dash of sugar. Every 20 minutes brush the top crust with it. This gives it a golden brown look.

Sweet Potato Pie

3 medium sweet potatoes, cooked, peeled while still warm
1 stick or ½ cup unsalted butter, room temperature
1 cup granulated sugar
¼ cup packed brown sugar
4 Medjool dates, soaked, pitted, and mashed
2 eggs
1 teaspoon each: vanilla and ground cinnamon
½ teaspoon each: ground nutmeg and allspice
9-inch unbaked pie crust

Preheat the oven to 350 degrees. Beat the sweet potatoes with an electric mixer on low speed while the potatoes are still warm. Add the butter; mix well. Beat in the sugars, dates, eggs, vanilla, cinnamon, nutmeg, and allspice; mix well. Pour into the pie crust. Bake until set and lightly brown on top, about 50–60 minutes; cool on wire rack at least 1 hour. Serves 8.

Sweet Potato Pone

3 pounds sweet potatoes
2 pounds sugar
2 (14-ounce) cans coconut milk
1 (14-ounce) can evaporated milk
¼ cup butter
1 tablespoon vanilla
¼ cup raisins
2 tablespoon grated ginger
pinch of ground nutmeg

Preheat oven to 350 degrees. Grate the sweet potatoes. Add the sugar and coconut milk. Stir until sugar dissolves, then add evaporated milk, butter, vanilla, and raisins. Stir until properly mixed and pour into a 9 x 11-inch baking pan. Bake for 45–60 minutes. Serves 10–12.

Cinnamon Rolls

2 cups milk
½ cup butter or margarine
½ cup sugar
4 eggs, beaten well
2 packages dry yeast
½ cup lukewarm water (dissolve the yeast in the warm water)
1 teaspoon salt
brown sugar butter
¼ cup good ground cinnamon

all-purpose flour
2 Medjool dates, soaked, pitted, and mashed

Preheat oven to 350 degrees. Scald milk. Add butter or margarine, and cool to lukewarm. Add sugar to well-beaten eggs, beat thoroughly, and add to warm milk. Add the dissolved yeast and salt. Add enough flour to make a smooth dough and knead well. Place the dough in a lightly greased bowl, cover, and let rise in a warm place until double in bulk (about 1 to 1½ hours). Roll out dough in a long strip (about 12 x 45 inches, if you want to get technical). Spread melted or soft butter or margarine over the dough. Add brown sugar to coat (be as generous as you like). Sprinkle with cinnamon. Roll up and cut into pieces with a sharp knife. For extra gooey rolls, put a piece of butter and cover with about ⅛ to ¼ cup of brown sugar on the pan where each cinnamon roll will be. Place the rolls on top of each pile of butter and sugar. (A pan with higher edges works best.) Bake for about 20 minutes. When you take the buns out of the oven, flip them on the gooey side and some of it will run down into the bun.

CROWD-PLEASING VEGAN DISHES

Kawaida Rice

(Courtesy of Omowale Kierstedt)

Kawaida Rice is a traditional recipe passed down through The East organization, and it was the hottest thing on the menu at The East Kitchen. Prepare the amount of rice you'd normally cook as a side dish to feed the number of guests you're expecting, and this recipe will yield a flavorful and attractive main dish that will stretch much further. The dish responds to each cook's creativity, as the ratio of veggies to rice or to other veggies is a matter of personal preference. There's only one imperative, says Omowale: Use fresh, not frozen, vegetables.

carrots, chopped
celery, sliced
green, red, and yellow sweet peppers, chopped
onions, white and red
scallions
white mushrooms
corn cut off the cob
cauliflower
broccoli
mung bean sprouts
zucchini
garlic
double-black sesame sauce or Bragg Liquid Aminos
oil
other seasonings to taste (oregano, basil, cumin, dried parsley, etc.)
medium- or long-grain brown or white rice, cooked 1 hour to ½ day ahead and cooled

Sauté vegetables with seasonings, adding quick-cooking veggies last (mushrooms, peppers, and sprouts). In a large wok or frying pan, add veggies to cooked rice in batches. Mix lightly to avoid sticky rice.

Gemi's Greens

1 large bunch collards
1 small bunch mustard greens
1 large red onion, chopped
1 medium white onion, chopped
2 cloves garlic, sliced
4 tablespoons safflower oil
Bragg Liquid Aminos to taste

Slice off stem tips of greens, leaving a generous amount of stem. Submerge greens in water in a large bowl or pot. Clean greens by hand in the water, removing sediment from leaves. Drain off water. Rinse sediment from bottom of bowl, and repeat. Drain and rinse greens a few times if necessary, until sediment is gone. Shake excess water from greens, separate into three or four bunches, and roll each bunch in a double length of sturdy paper towel. Squeeze gently to remove remaining water. Unwrap bundles of greens and slice each horizontally into medium-sized strips.

Sauté onions and garlic in oil for 1 minute. Add a few handfuls of sliced greens and sauté lightly for 1 minute until greens begin to limp. Gradually add the remainder of the greens, a few handfuls at a time. When all greens are limp, sauté together for another 2 minutes, then add Bragg Aminos and 1½ to 2 cups of water or enough to cook greens, leaving a little stock. Add water if necessary while cooking on a medium, then low flame for 25 minutes or so, according to how tender you prefer your greens. Remove from heat.

Dafuah's Delish Seitan Dish

2 cups dehydrated shiitake mushrooms or 2 large portabella mushrooms
1 large onion, chopped or sliced
2 cloves fresh garlic, pressed
safflower oil as needed (a little)
2 cups water
stock from seitan containers
2 tablespoons roasted tahini
2 1-pound containers of seitan (wheat gluten), cut in medium-sized pieces
1 each: small red, green, and yellow sweet bell pepper
freshly ground cumin to taste
Bragg Liquid Aminos to taste
4 or 5 fresh basil leaves or ½ teaspoon dried basil
½ teaspoon dried marjoram
½ teaspoon dried chives
a pinch of dried oregano
a few stalks cilantro, chopped

Preheat oven to 400 degrees.

Break shiitake mushrooms in half, cracking the caps. Soak in hot water until soft, then drain and squeeze lightly to expel excess water. If using fresh mushrooms, cut portabellas into ½-inch slices. Sauté onion and garlic in safflower oil in a cast-iron skillet (if possible). When limp, add water, seitan stock, and tahini. Add remaining ingredients, cover, bring to a light boil, and simmer a few moments until stock thickens into gravy, stirring occasionally. Transfer to a roasting pan and bake for 30 minutes. Serve over rice or pasta. Serves 8.

Vegan Mac and "Cheese"

4 cups pasta, cooked
1 package (10 ounces) Follow Your Heart Gourmet Cheese Alternative (Cheddar)
½ cup unsweetened original-flavored soy or rice milk (not vanilla)
1 teaspoon mild mustard (not powdered)
5 teaspoons nutritional yeast
2 tablespoons vegan margarine (nonhydrogenated)
2 teaspoons garlic powder
a pinch of paprika
finely ground sea salt or Bragg Liquid Aminos to taste
pepper to taste

Preheat oven to 350 degrees.

Cook pasta and set aside. Cook all other ingredients on low flame in a sauce pot, stirring consistently until melted and thick. Add more soy or rice milk if needed. Place pasta in a bowl and mix in three-quarters of cheese sauce. Place in a casserole dish and pour remaining cheese sauce on top. Sprinkle paprika lightly over top. Bake for 15 minutes.

Sasteh's Slammin' Tofu

Tofu

2 pounds tofu, drained and sliced
Bragg Liquid Aminos
2 cups all-purpose flour
1 cup finely ground cornmeal
a pinch each of curry, onion powder, garlic powder, and dried thyme

Marinate sliced tofu 1 hour in Bragg Aminos to cover. Combine flour, cornmeal, and spices for breading. Drain tofu and pat dry, then bread each slice. Deep-fry in vegetable oil until light brown. (For a lower-fat version of this recipe, grill the tofu with fat-free butter spray instead of frying.)

Gravy

2 medium onions, coarsely chopped
3 tablespoons extra virgin olive oil or other light oil
Bragg Liquid Aminos
a pinch each: onion, curry, and garlic powder
a pinch each: black pepper and dried basil
⅓ cup all-purpose flour
1 cup water
½ cup barbecue sauce

Preheat oven to 350 degrees. Sauté chopped onions in ½ cup water until limp. Add Bragg Aminos, oil, spices, and barbecue sauce. Add flour and ½ cup water, gradually. Stir into gravy.

Arrange sliced, fried tofu in rows in a 13 x 9-inch baking pan. Cover with gravy, cover pan with foil, and bake for 20 to 30 minutes.

Vegetarian Chili

1 tablespoon olive oil
1 medium onion, chopped
4 cloves garlic, minced
½ pound mushrooms, chopped
2 cups cauliflower pieces
1 large potato, peeled and diced
1 large green pepper, seeded and chopped
2 large carrots, chopped

3 cups corn kernels
8 plum tomatoes, chopped
4 cups cooked kidney beans
1 cup tomato juice
2 stalks celery, chopped
1 tablespoon cumin
2 tablespoons chili powder
1 teaspoon paprika
1½ teaspoons salt
⅛ teaspoon cayenne pepper
2 tablespoons tomato paste

Heat olive oil in a large stew pot. Add onion and garlic and sauté until onion is wilted, about 5 minutes. Add mushrooms and sauté another 10 minutes. Stir in cauliflower, potato, green pepper, carrots, corn, tomatoes, beans, tomato juice, celery, all seasonings, and tomato paste. Bring to a boil. Reduce heat and simmer. Cover and cook until vegetables are tender, about 30 minutes. You can add more spices if you like it hotter.

Curry Cornbread

1 cup yellow cornmeal
1 cup whole wheat pastry flour
1 tablespoon baking powder
½ teaspoon mild curry powder
¼ teaspoon sea salt
½ cup canola oil
2 tablespoons maple syrup
1 cup water

Preheat oven to 350 degrees. In separate bowls, mix the dry and the wet ingredients. Add the dry ingredients to the wet ones and stir until well combined. Pour into an oiled 9-inch round or square baking pan. Bake for 30 minutes. Cool and serve. Serves 9.

Maitefa's Vegan Macaroni Salad

2 boxes DeBoles Organic Elbow-Style Pasta or other
2 medium red bell peppers, chopped
2 medium yellow bell peppers, chopped (use green if unavailable)
1 medium red onion, chopped
1 medium white onion, chopped
4 stalks celery, diced
1 pound cooked tofu (optional)
2 tablespoons nutritional yeast
Bragg Liquid Aminos to taste or finely ground sea salt
dried parsley to taste
dried chives to taste
1 jar Cascadian Farms organic sweet relish
1 16 oz. jar Follow Your Heart Vegenaise (use more or less, to taste)
dash of paprika
4 sprigs fresh parsley, chopped

Cook the macaroni with a little oil in the water. Drain and cool completely at room temperature in a large colander with a plate beneath to catch the last of the water. Place in the freezer for 10 minutes, stirring once, or in the refrigerator for 20 minutes, stirring once. While the pasta is cooling, chop the veggies and cube the cooked tofu, if using. Add the nutritional yeast, Bragg Aminos, or sea salt to pasta once cooled. Add chopped veggies, dried parsley, dried chives, relish, and tofu. Add Vegenaise, mixing well, but lightly. Sprinkle the top with paprika and garnish with chopped parsley.

East Africa: Kachumbari (A Spicy Cole Slaw)

1 hot chili pepper, cleaned, seeds removed, chopped
1 medium onion, chopped
2 to 4 tomatoes, thinly sliced
juice of 1–2 lemons or limes
½ to 1 teaspoon salt
a few pinches fresh cilantro, chopped
1 cucumber, peeled and sliced
1 small cabbage, shredded

Combine all ingredients in a mixing bowl. Toss to coat all ingredients with liquid. Set aside in a cool place for 20 to 30 minutes before serving. Eat within 12 hours.

Zanzibar: Plantains in Coconut Milk

4 or more plantains
½ teaspoon mild curry powder
½ teaspoon cinnamon (optional)
a few cloves or a pinch of powdered cloves (optional)
salt to taste
1 to 2 cups coconut milk

Peel plantains and cut into slices or quarters. In a saucepan, combine all ingredients except coconut milk. Heat slowly, stir gently, and add coconut milk little by little, until all is absorbed. Simmer until plantains are tender. Add a little water if necessary.

Ner Enen's Tropical Fruit Crisp

1 20-ounce can unsweetened pineapple chunks with juice drained off
2 large ripe bananas cut in ½-inch chunks
2 tablespoons dried grated coconut
½ teaspoon ground cinnamon
a large pinch of fresh grated nutmeg
2 tablespoons sweetened pineapple juice
½ teaspoon light rum
1 cup of your favorite granola or chopped nuts

Position rack in center of oven and preheat to 350 degrees. In an 8-inch square baking dish, place the pineapples and bananas. Sprinkle with coconut, cinnamon, and nutmeg, and toss to blend. Pour pineapple juice and rum over fruit and sprinkle granola or nuts on top. Bake uncovered for 25 minutes. Serve warm by itself or with ice cream or whipped cream. Serves about 4.

SOMETHING FOR EVERYONE: RAW FOOD RECIPES

Raw Soul's Holiday Pâté

½ cup sunflower seeds, soaked and sprouted
½ cup almonds, soaked and peeled

½ cup walnuts, soaked
6 sun-dried tomatoes
1 tablespoon Italian seasoning
2 gloves garlic
1 tablespoon paprika
1 tablespoon dried parsley
1 tablespoon pizza herbs
½ red onion, diced
½ cup fresh cilantro
water from sun-dried tomatoes

Combine all ingredients in a food processor. Blend well to a chunky consistency. Serve with crackers, or roll on a sheet of nori or a collard leaf. Cut stem from leaf. Place pâté in leaf. Top with sprouts. Roll. Refrigerate up to 1 week. Serves 4.

Raw Soul's Lip-Smacking Yams

¼ cup dates, soaked 20 minutes, pitted and coarsely chopped
¼ cup raisins, soaked 20 minutes
¼ cup pine nuts, soaked 5–10 minutes
3 small yams, peeled and cut in chunks
2 tablespoons cinnamon
2 tablespoons allspice
2 tablespoons garam masala

Soak the dates, raisins, and pine nuts in three separate bowls. Peel and cut the yams. Place yams, dates, raisins, and pine nuts in Vita-Mix or food processor and blend to a coarse consistency. Transfer the mixture to a bowl and add seasonings. Mix well. Adjust flavors as necessary. Serve immediately or refrigerate up to 1 week. Serves 4.

Mawule's Ocean Dumplings with Sweet and Spicy Sauce

Dumplings

1 cup Brazil nuts, soaked 8 hours in spring water to cover
1 cup almonds, soaked 8 hours in spring water to cover
8 sheets of nori, cut in four squares each
½ cup hijiki seaweed broken into small pieces
1 cup wakame seaweed broken into small pieces
½ cup arame seaweed broken into small pieces
¼ cup lemon juice
¼ cup extra virgin olive oil
½ cup nama shoyu or Bragg Liquid Aminos
½ teaspoon ground black pepper
1 tablespoon paprika
a pinch each of cayenne and fine-ground sea salt to taste
¼ cup dulse flakes
3 stalks celery, chopped fine
1 scallion, chopped
1 small stem of cilantro, chopped

Spread nuts on paper towels to air dry. Marinate seaweeds for 15 minutes or until soft in lemon juice, oil, nama shoyu or Bragg's Amino, pepper, paprika, cayenne, and salt. Set aside.

In a food processor with the S-blade, place the Brazil nuts and almonds. Blend on high to puree to a fine consistency. Remove and place in a bowl. Add dulse flakes, chopped celery, scallion, cilantro, and marinated seaweed. Return to food processor and pulse four or five times to blend. If mixture is too thick, add a little more olive oil, nama shoyu, or Bragg's. Place 1 tablespoon in center of each nori square. Bring the corners of the square together to make a bundle. Pinch edges together and seal with a few drops of lemon juice. Set aside to air dry.

Dipping Sauce
1 teaspoon ground mustard seed
¼ cup apple cider vinegar
⅛ teaspoon ground turmeric
¼ cup lemon juice
¼ cup olive oil
¼ to ½ cup hulled (white) sesame seeds
4 Medjool dates pitted
1 clove garlic
a pinch of cayenne pepper (optional)

Blend all ingredients in a Vita-Mix or other on highest speed to creamy consistency. Serve at room temperature or slightly chilled with dumplings.

Maitefa's Marinated Greens with Sweet Peppers

3 bunches organic lacinto kale
2 limes
organic safflower oil
Bragg Liquid Aminos or finely ground sea salt, or both
2 large red bell peppers
2 medium yellow bell peppers
1 large red onion

Wash and pat-dry kale. Run a small, sharp knife along one and then the other side of the leaf's spine and remove it. Set leaves aside in a large bowl, squeeze limes, and add their juice to the bowl, mixing lightly. Add a tablespoon or more of oil, a little sea salt, and Bragg Aminos. Use scrubbed-clean hands (plastic gloves optional) to massage lime juice, salt, and oil into the greens for 2 minutes. Cut the peppers into medium-thin strips, slice the onion into thin rings, and add to the greens. Massage for 1 minute more. Taste and adjust if needed. Cover bowl and let sit out for up to 2 hours, then toss lightly and refrigerate. (If it's hot in the kitchen, refrigerate after 1 hour.) Marinate in refrigerator overnight, tossing once before bed and once in the morning, or eat right away if preferred; the longer the marinating process, the more tender and flavorful the greens.

Optional: Slice the meat from the pit of eight Black Cerignola olives, cut into smaller strips, and add to greens before marinating. Also can add kernels cut from two ears of fresh raw corn.

RAW DESSERTS

Raw Soul's Fruit Parfait

meat from 1 young coconut
½ cup cashews
1 teaspoon vanilla extract (alcohol-free)
4 tablespoons lime juice
2 tablespoons raw honey
¼ cup coconut water
½ cup pecans, chopped
½ cup raisins
2 cups of mixed fruit (blueberries, pineapple, strawberries, etc.)

Combine the coconut meat, cashews, vanilla, lime juice, honey, and coconut water in blender. Blend on high until creamy. Layer cream, nuts, and fruit in a serving cup or bowl. Repeat. Refrigerate. Serves 2.

Mawule's Macaroons with Strawberry Centers

1 cup almonds, soaked and dried
1 cup macadamia nuts, soaked and dried
¼ teaspoon coarsely ground sea salt
1 cup Medjool dates, pitted
2 tablespoons natural vanilla extract
2 tablespoons almond extract
1 cup dried white coconut, grated
½ cup raw honey or agave nectar

Put almonds, macadamia nuts, and salt in a food processor with the S-blade. Grind until fine. Add dates and blend well. Add vanilla and almond extracts and process until well mixed. Remove from processor and place in a large bowl. Add dried coconut and honey or agave nectar. Put on a pair of disposable plastic gloves and knead the mixture until stiff. Roll into balls and place on a baking sheet. Flatten balls with a spoon into ½ inch–thick patties. Make a round depression in center of each pattie and set aside to air dry.

Fruit Center
1 cup fresh strawberries
8 Medjool dates, pitted
a pinch of finely ground sea salt

Blend all ingredients in a Vita-Mix on high speed until jam consistency. Fill the center of each macaroon with jam and refrigerate for 30 minutes. Should make approximately 18 macaroons.

Simply Amazing Raw Chocolate Pudding

4 ripe Hass avocadoes or 3 of a larger variety
6 to 8 Medjool dates to taste
Shiloh Farms Organic Cocoa Powder (to taste)
spring, distilled, or filtered water

Remove pits from dates and soak in water to cover for 5 minutes. Remove skin and pits from avocadoes, cut into large pieces, and place in food processor with the S-blade or in a blender. Drain and chop soaked dates. Add enough date water to avocadoes to allow for processing or blending. Run on high speed for 30 seconds. Add 1 or more tablespoons of cocoa powder through lid opening and run for another 30 seconds. Add chopped dates through lid and run for 1 minute. Taste to determine if additional cocoa powder or sweetener is needed and if desired consistency has been reached. Complete to taste.

Sources

Lillian Butler and Eddie Robinson, the husband-and-wife proprietors of Raw Soul, can be reached at their restaurant at 348 West 145th Street, Harlem, New York, (212) 491-5859. Order their book, *Raw Soul: Just Desserts*, their cookies, and other items at www.rawsoul.com.

Mawule Jobe-Simon, proprietor of the former Green Paradise restaurant in Brooklyn, New York, operates a raw food chef service and will soon make his famous spicy veggie crackers available in stores. He can be reached for further information at (347) 683-8997.

The African recipes here can be found along with hundreds of others at www.congocookbook.com. The Caribbean Rice and Beans recipe was adapted from a Web site promoting Nevis tourism. See www.nevis1.com/index.html. Find lots of great vegetarian recipes at www.blackvegetarians.com and at groups.msn.com/VegetarianSOULFOOD/soulvegetarianrecipes.msnw.

Cascadian Farms, Shiloh Farms, and Follow Your Heart products are available at most health food stores. If they're not in your area, however, reach the companies directly at their Web sites: www.smallplanetfoods.com, www.celiac.com/catalog/product, and www.followyourheart.com.

Chapter Seven

Kwanzaa Songs Carry the Message

HERE are ten Kwanzaa songs and one Kwanzaa rap you can use to help make your ceremony and celebration joyful. Many are call-and-response in the African tradition, all are user-friendly for children, and some were designed for the very young to learn with ease.

This first song is known to celebrants of Kwanzaa the world over and is believed to have originated at The East cultural center in Brooklyn, New York.

KWANZAA IS A HOLIDAY
By Imani Duckett-Gibbs

Kwanzaa is a holiday
Kwanzaa, Kwanzaa, Kwanzaa is an African holiday
Seven principles, seven candles
Seven special days for Africans!
(*Repeat*)

Children love to sing this next one, which invokes spelling, along with their parents or other adults.

KWANZAA WIMBO

By Sayeed Amon Ra

Call-and-response, with response in italics.

I said-a hey, hey, hey! Kwanzaa's here to stay!
(I said-a hey, hey, hey! Kwanzaa's here to stay!)
I said-a hey, hey, HEY! Kwanzaa's here to stay!
(I said-a hey, hey, HEY! Kwanzaa's here to stay!)

I said, Boom, boom, boom! I'm gonna break it down for you
Boom, boom, boom! I'm gonna break it down for you
I said, Boom, boom, boom! Let me break it down for you
Boom, boom, boom! Let me break it down for you

K stands for Kings, mighty, mighty Kings
W stands for Woman, proud Black Woman
A stands for Africa, sweet mother Africa
N stands for nation, proud Black nation
Z stands for zawadi, the gift of love
A stands for all, all Black folks in love, I said—
A stands for all, all Black folks in love

Now you get it, now you got it
This is what it means
Kwanzaa—seven holy days of the year!

NGUZO SABA

Arranged by Yusef Iman

Call-and-response, with response in italics, to a swing-time beat.

We need Umoja!
Umoja
Because it's Unity!
'Cause it's Unity!
(Repeat all 4 lines)
We need Kujichagulia!
Kujichagulia!
Self-determination!
Self-determination!
(Repeat all 4)
We need Ujima!
Ujima!
Collective work and responsibility!
Collective work and responsibility!
(Repeat last 2)
We need Ujamaa!
Ujamaa!
Cooperative economics!
Cooperative economics!
(Repeat all 4)
Nia!
Nia!
Purpose!
Purpose!
Kuumba!
Kuumba!

Creativity!
Creativity!
Imani!
Imani!
Faith!
Faith!

Faith in our Blackness
Faith in our Blackness
We need faith in our Blackness
Faith in our Blackness
We need faith in our parents
Faith in our parents
Faith in our children
Faith in our children
Faith in our teachers
Faith in our teachers
Faith in our leaders
Faith in our leaders
Faith in ourselves!
Faith in ourselves!

This one is not formally a Kwanzaa song, but is a standard for long-time Kwanzaa celebrants on the East Coast of the United States. It offers an interpretation of the colors of the bendera and was sung by students at Uhuru Sasa school in the 1970s.

PRAISE THE RED, THE BLACK AND THE GREEN

By Yusef Iman

Call-and-response, with response in italics.

Chorus (all together)
Praise the Red, the Black and the Green
Brothers and sisters we're being redeemed
Open up your eyes and see
We're on our way to being free!

Because red is for the blood that we shed
Red is for the blood that we shed
Black is for the race—that's us!
Black is for the race—that's us!
Green is for the land, uh huh
Green is for the land, uh huh
Where the Black folks can take their rightful place
Where the Black folks can take their rightful place
(Chorus)
I said, praise the Red, the Black and the Green
Brothers and sisters we're being redeemed
Open up your eyes and see
We're on our way to being free!
(Repeat entire song.)

Simple and motivating, this next Kwanzaa song is another by the masterful Yusef Iman.

KWANZAA!

By Yusef Iman

Kwanzaa, a step to liberation
Kwanzaa, a step to our nation
Kwanzaa helps us to see
That we are in control of our own destiny!
Kwanzaa, a step for you and me
Kwanzaa, for us to be free
Kwanzaa helps us to see
That we are in control of our own destiny!
Kwanzaa!

KWANZAA IS AN AFRICAN FEAST (THE KWANZAA CALYPSO)

By Yusef Waliyaya

Kwanzaa, Kwanzaa is an African feast
Kwanzaa, Kwanzaa is an African feast
Kwanzaa, Kwanzaa is an African feast
For all our people!

Kwanzaa, Kwanzaa we sing and dance
Kwanzaa, Kwanzaa we sing and dance
Kwanzaa, Kwanzaa we sing and dance
For all our people!

Kwanzaa, Kwanzaa we sing and dance
Kwanzaa, Kwanzaa we sing and dance
Kwanzaa, Kwanzaa we sing and dance
In praise of the Creator!

This song was included in a play entitled *What Iza Kwanzaa?* by Yusef Waliyaya, "The Kwanzaa Griot."

HEY, THIS IS KWANZAA!
By Yusef Waliyaya

Kwanzaa is the harvest for the children of the sun
Seven days of learning and a lot of fun
Kwanzaa is the colors red, black and green
Kwanzaa, holy days made for kings and queens

Everybody say—
"Hey, this is Kwanzaa!
Hey, this is Kwanzaa
(3 calls, 3 responses)
Look at our ceremonies
Sing our song of glee
Lighting of the candles
Make it fun for you and me
Pass around the unity cup
And drink it right up
Seven African holy days here in America
Enjoy them now before they're gone
Remember this is Kwanzaa

Everybody say—
"Hey, this is Kwanzaa!
Hey, this is Kwanzaa
(3 calls, 3 responses)

At the time this one was written, Kwanzaa was not as widely celebrated. This short song is repeated several times, scatting and swinging a few of the lines for a jazzy groove.

KWANZAA BLUES
By Yusef Waliyaya

Nobody knows about Kwanzaa
K-W-A-N-Z-A-A
Nobody knows about Kwanzaa
Kwanzaa holiday, on the way

Take time to learn about Kwanzaa
It's African just like you
Well you know that it's time for Kwanzaa
Are you gonna know what to do?
Are you gonna know what to do?

This is another song performed in Waliyaya's play and at numerous Kwanzaa presentations.

AIN'T IT GREAT?
By Yusef Waliyaya

Kwanzaa is a time for unity
Kwanzaa is a time for community
Kwanzaa is a time to celebrate
The fruits of our labor
Now ain't that great?
Now ain't that great?

Have love for your mother, father, sisters and brothers
Always respect your ancestral mother

Concentrate on work, there'll be time for play
Propagate the legacy of Kwanzaa today

Ain't it great?
To celebrate, celebrate Kwanzaa!
Celebrate, celebrate Kwanzaa!
Celebrate, celebrate Kwanzaa!
Celebrate, celebrate Kwanzaa!

KWANZAA

By Atiba Kwabena Wilson

Written as a rap for *Kwanzaa Suite,* a 1998 stage production, this is great for memorizing the meanings of the Seven Principles. It is used by permission of the author.

Knowledge is key to reach understandin'
Wisdom is to use it / Calls for greater plannin'
Ancestors guide us each and every day
Nguzo Saba are the rules of the way
Zimbabwe, Guinea, Angola, Sudan
Africa's a continent shonuff grand!
Kwanzaa represents the fruits of the year
A harvest party that helps us be clear
Umoja is Oneness spirit and mind
Everybody growin' flowin' in time
Kujichagulia means self-determination
Thinkin' for ourselves without hesitation
Ujima is work, responsibility
To help maintain, build the community
U-ja-maa talks about money
Everyone shares, we all taste honey

Nia means purpose (in other words, goal . . .)
Keepin' us focused, movin' as a whole
Kuumba is sound creativity
Addin' to the beauty of reality
Imani is faith, we need to begin
Believe in our people, struggle to win

Kwanzaa is a harvest celebratin' time
It's not just a party, it's freein' up your mind
Kwanzaa is a harvest celebratin' time
It's not just a party, it's freein' up your mind!

Featuring a mellow reggae tempo, the following song is one of several on Kwanzaa Kwest Products' *Nguzo Saba* CD. The song is available for free download at kwanzaamedia.com, where a video is also available.

THE KWANZAA SONG
By Okera Ras I

This is a song about Kwanzaa
We tell you this is a song about Kwanzaa
This is a song about Kwanzaa
We tell you this is a song about Kwanzaa

Now this is a message for everybody
Me say you, your brethren, your sistren and your family
The word Kwanzaa means First Fruits in Kiswahili
It's a special time for you and me
It's from December 26th to the first of January
A time to reaffirm our values and our identity

And fight the negative results of slavery
It started 1966 by Maulana Karenga
I tell you that Jah man he was a professor
He teach Black studies in the California
The roots of Kwanzaa come from Africa
Now we the Africans in the Diaspora
We pull upon this energy so we can prosper
That's the Seven Principles called the Nguzo Saba

Principle number one—Umoja
Principle number two—Kujichagulia
Principle number three—Ujima
Principle number four—Ujamaa
Principle number five—the one, Nia
Principle number six—Kuumba
Number seven you see, is called Imani

We tell you this is a song about Kwanzaa
We tell you this is a song about Kwanzaa—Right!
This is a song about Kwanzaa
This is a song about Kwanzaa
Ah me say—
Kwanzaa Kwanzaa Kwanzaa Kwanzaa
Kwanzaa Kwanzaa Kwanzaa Kwanzaa
Kwanzaa Kwanzaa Kwanzaa Kwanzaa
Kwanzaa Kwanzaa Kwanzaa Kwanzaa
(Repeat second stanza.)
This is a song about Kwanzaa (4X)
Kwanzaa Kwanzaa Kwanzaa Kwanzaa (4X)
We come fi nice it up ina Kwanzaa stylee . . .

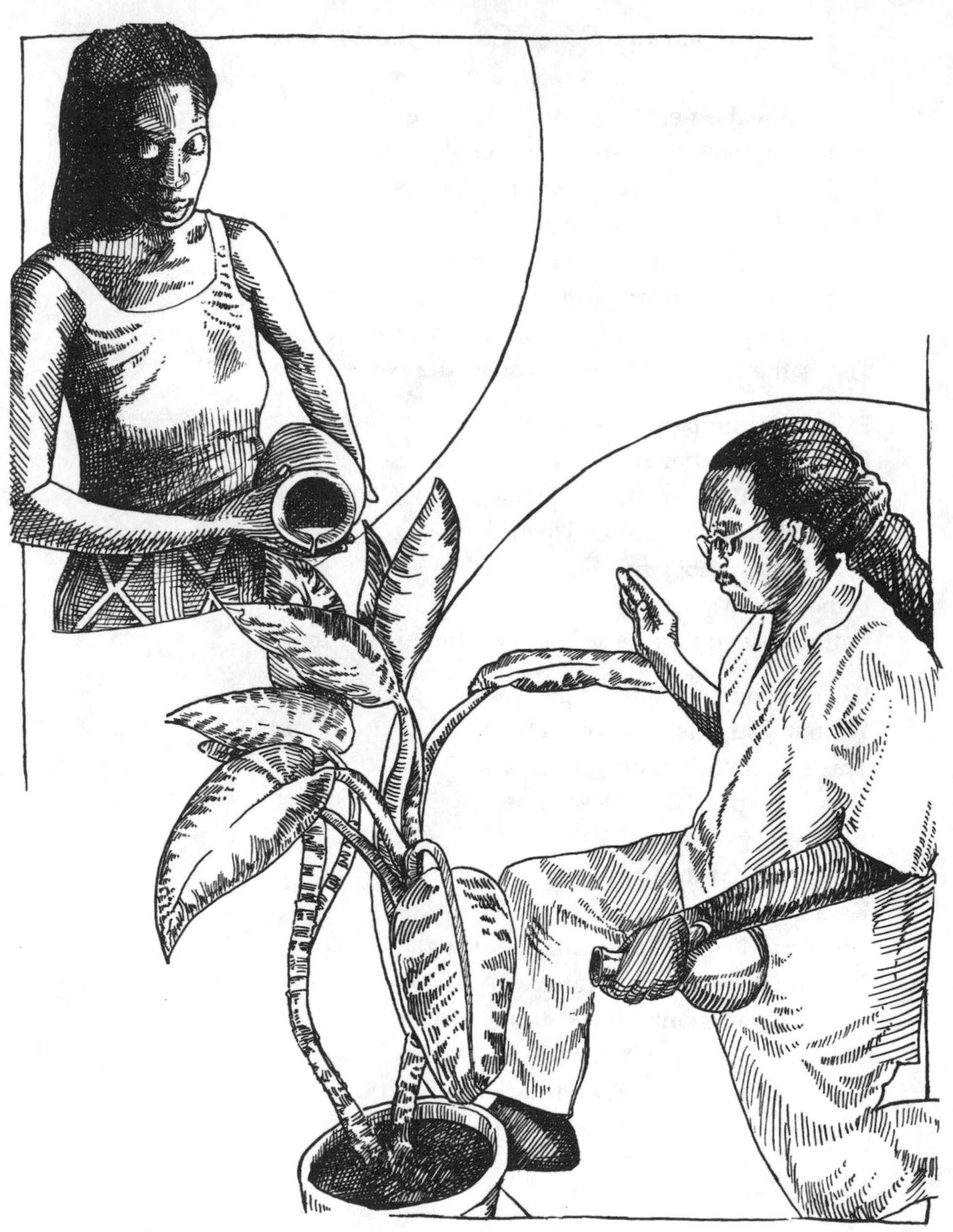

Chapter Eight

Living and Working Kwanzaa All Year

KWANZAA is a wonderful, inspiration-filled week. In giving thanks for those first fruits, we accept the responsibility to make productive use of our blessings. Just as the traditional harvest feasts celebrated a year's worth of work and its rewards, Kwanzaa is intended to help us take stock of the work we've done. The implication is that we'll rededicate ourselves to those thoughts and actions that caused us to flourish, and move away from those that threatened or hindered our progress.

In order to be successful in doing this, we need to stop relegating Kwanzaa to just one week of the year and make it a year-round frame of reference for concerted effort, culminating in a celebration and rededication. Offered below are some actions that can help us to do this. They are not sweeping societal prescriptions or political directives, but a few suggestions that focus on the small things each individual can do within their own sphere of activity. Again, most readers have valuable insights of their own that will translate into small, achievable actions or even larger, collective ones that can positively impact the community. You'll also find here examples of inspiring individuals or groups involved in activity related to a particular principle. We hope that all of this material will aid you in your attempts to stay principled beyond the holiday.

Umoja 365—A Daily Commitment to Unity

❋ Join an organization. Don't rationalize apathy with, "I'm just not a joiner!" If you're not, fine—then start something. A unified front will usually beat a solo effort, whether it's advocating for high-performing schools, organizing for economic opportunity, or electing a candidate who'll represent the group's interests with energy and integrity. First do a little research on an organization you're interested in, and if you're commitment-shy, start small, with a block association, for example. If you find that's honestly all you can manage, then stick with that, but if you can do more, move on to volunteering occasionally to help further a cause that's close to your heart. If you find you're becoming passionate about it and the organization is the right fit, then join.

❋ Be a peacekeeper in your home—that's where Umoja truly begins. Try to defuse arguments when possible, or at the very least, refuse to contribute to their escalation. In a family setting, it's almost always your business, but if it's not, encourage the parties involved in the conflict to come to a peaceful resolution and then retreat to a respectful distance where you can be easily reached if needed. Of course, if the parties involved are children, teach them conflict resolution skills and know that you will most likely have to intervene. When you do, try your best not to show favoritism.

❋ Have regular family meetings—once a month works for most families, while others prefer a brief meeting each week. Family meetings are a great vehicle for sharing news, resolving minor grievances, and asking for needed support. Children are especially benefited by the model of cooperation presented, and they get to know the adults in a more meaningful way. Use family meetings to also discuss more mundane matters, such as chores, financial priorities, and vacation plans. You'll find that things will run more smoothly from month to month.

❋ Get together with your family members to have fun that has nothing to do with errands, paying bills, or household duties. If this means you have to find extra time, try to find it. Get up earlier to exercise or meditate together. Rent a movie, see a play, or read the same book at the same time and discuss it afterward at a family picnic. Schedule a game night at regular intervals, and make sure everyone is given enough notice to make it a priority item on the calendar. Go on vacation or on a day trip. Be adventurous—if rock climbing is a bit ambitious, start by ordering something different from the take-out menu! Experiencing new things together helps a couple, family, or group to bond.

❋ Seek assistance from a support group if you or a family member has been impacted by a serious challenge such as a disability, an addiction, a history of abuse, or an identity crisis. Once the butt of jokes, support circles have earned a reputation as arenas where real work can get done. Choose wisely, and if you're not impressed with the choices in your area, consider online support groups, again choosing carefully. Not only can you obtain assistance, but your participation and perspective may help another in your situation.

❋ Reach across class, gender, and political lines to acknowledge the common challenges we face. You may not hang out with the brothers on the corner, but you can speak when you pass by each evening. When you're on the receiving end of service, make sure to acknowledge the provider. Exchange greetings with the man mopping the halls at your office building, and ask the name of the woman who brings fresh towels to your hotel room. On another equally important note: Men and women of African descent can't spare the time or energy it takes to hold grudges against an entire opposite sex, to call names, or to otherwise disrespect one another. Finally, don't become too comfortable or complacent to acknowledge the right of others to organize around the issues that most immediately affect them.

❋ Cherish and celebrate young people who are putting in work to better our condition. The widespread stereotypes of Black youth are just that, and we should know better than to buy into the same type of disparagement long directed at people of African descent as a whole. We can't effectively stem fratricide among young Black males in many urban areas, for example, until we acknowledge that many more are keeping themselves productively occupied. What are the differences between the two groups? How can we replicate the positive factors?

❋ Support newlyweds and new parents. Oftentimes they won't reach out for help because they don't want to be dictated to or judged. If you've been there, make your experience count for something by using it in service of those who don't have a track record. You just might make the difference for a young husband and wife hoping to one day celebrate their fiftieth wedding anniversary. Before you jump in, however, offer your assistance first, in a low-pressure manner, so that you're not intruding where you're not welcome. In most cases you'll be surprised at how eagerly your offer to babysit or to discuss relationship strategies over dinner is accepted. If not, move on and offer help elsewhere. Of course, you won't expect a young couple to hand their baby or their dilemmas over to you if they don't really know you, and don't be offended if they follow some advice while declining some.

❋ Practice Umoja by refusing to bad-mouth other people. If someone approaches with gossip, decline to participate. If you say anything, offer words of understanding rather than disparagement. The considerable work we have to do can be facilitated if we can trust one another. Be a tolerant influence in your family and circle of friends. Be the voice of reason if your committee gets bogged down in disputes while seeking to organize around an issue. Follow the advice your parents gave concerning matters that don't directly affect you: if you don't have anything nice to say, don't say anything at all.

Umoja Works

❋ Tamika Chatman of Brooklyn, New York, has used Kwanzaa to bring her family together—literally. Chatman's family life was interrupted in childhood when her mother's drug use led to Tamika and her three siblings being separated and placed in kinship care with relatives and a godmother. Although those who took them in were well intentioned, Tamika seldom saw her brother and sisters.

Tamika's now thirty-six, her siblings are adults (one passed away at age twenty-two), and her mother no longer uses drugs. Four years ago Tamika invited family members to join her in celebrating her first Kwanzaa. It was a meaningful celebration for all and has become an annual gathering. Using the Nguzo Saba as a roadmap, the siblings now meet regularly to discuss the progress of common objectives set at the Kwanzaa ceremony. One year they traced their lineage and created a family tree. Two years ago, with her family's support, Tamika lost seventy pounds and the siblings are working on buying property together and opening a family business. "Kwanzaa started the chain reaction," Tamika says. "You need all the pieces of the puzzle to make it."

❋ John Watusi Branch of the Afrikan Poetry Theatre (APT) of Queens, New York, knows what it's like to be on the receiving end of an Umoja initiative. The Theatre, which he founded thirty years ago along with the late Yusef Waliyaya, began as an ensemble seeking to "spread the word and raise consciousness" through poetry, song, jazz, blues, and African music. Two years later, APT had a physical home and began building a roster of programs that today includes poetry workshops, plays, music and language instruction, lectures, mentoring, and summer employment and career exploration programs for youth. APT also produces what's come to be known as a "must-make" Kwanzaa celebration, hosting close to 1,000 people each year at a full-day event often held at York College. It features a marketplace with about sixty vendors, a great lineup of talent, the lighting of a specially made giant kinara, and the distribution of fruit to the families and gifts to the children.

In 2002 fire destroyed one-quarter of the building housing APT. There was extensive water damage and five rooms were destroyed. Branch kept the faith as the Theatre navigated a bureaucratic maze of local politics in getting help to rebuild. Soon local community groups, including Cemotap (The Committee to Eliminate Media Offensive to

African People), the Jamaica Arts Center, and the Harvest Room came to the rescue, offering financial support and temporary space to house some APT programs. Branch and his staffers have persevered through trying times. Their spirits were bolstered by the support of the community, which contributed $140,000 to the rebuilding effort. At the time of the fire, APT was a vulnerable tenant. Today, it is a proud owner of the building that will serve as home base for the execution of its ambitious plans for the future. (Visit www.afrikapoetrytheatre.com.)

❋ Shepsu Day is an annual gathering that brings together people of various spiritual traditions who honor the ancestors in their daily lives. People unfamiliar with these traditions make the mistake of assuming they are monolithic, but they are not. Those who adhere to the Akan tradition of West Africa, for example, do some things differently from those who live by the Yoruba or Kemetic systems of belief. Each of these traditions and others hold valuable pieces of the mosaic of spiritual wisdom, and from time to time, some adherents express the desire to come together in a significant way.

In 1995 a group of observers in the Kemetic tradition hosted an ancestral celebration in New York City and invited members of other spiritual communities to join them in a libation ceremony, song, and dance. The gathering was a joyful success and Shepsu Day has become an annual October event which has featured the participation of a Zulu priest and representatives of the Taino tradition of Central America and the Diorhle people of Côte d'Ivoire, to name a few. The gathering has grown to be celebrated in Tulsa, Oklahoma, and London, England. Similarly, in 1998, the National African Religion Congress hosted its first conference in Philadelphia, which has gone on to become a great success, and the first Symposium on Indigenous African Spiritual Traditions was held in New York City in April 2006. These initiatives in the service of Umoja are in keeping with the pivotal principles of African tradition. (See www.shepsuday.org, www.narcworld.com, and www.africanspirituality.org).

❋ Onnie Millar is an eighty-seven-year-old Brooklyn-based artist and retired arts educator cherished as much for her warmth and wit as she is for her fascinating paintings, illustrations, and found-art creations. Her recollection of a meaningful time in her life illustrates the importance of making sure that elders remain an integral part of our lives. A truly unified society includes and is enriched by the contributions of its elders; feeling valued helps elders to lead more fulfilling lives.

"I remember meeting and being invited into the lives of some younger artists," Millar says, "and we learned from one another. We watched how they spoke to and interacted with their children and raised them in beautiful, fearless ways. That was so interesting to us older artists who had raised children decades earlier. Damali Miller, one younger artist with whom I worked, would have a special dinner when her child or a relative's child was going off to college. Everyone would speak to the child that was leaving, giving some advice. What got you was the interest on the part of the young people and I felt that I learned so much, as well. You really felt tied in to the family and invested in what was going to happen with these young people and you followed their progress through those college years."

❋ Leroy Moore is an outspoken disabled man of African descent living in California. He is a poet, columnist, activist, radio host and performer, and creator of a lecture series entitled "On the Outskirts:

Race and Disability." Moore is founder and chair of Disability Advocates of Minorities (DAMU) and of New Voices: Disabled Poets of Color. His work is included in the collection *Molotov Mouths* and he performs with the Molotov Mouths: Outspoken Word Troupe. He pens a column, "Illin 'N Chillin'," for poormagazine.com and released a spoken-word recording, *Black Disabled Man with a Big Mouth & a High IQ*. Moore has traveled to London, Canada, and South Africa lecturing on racism and ablism, sexuality, disabled Black people in history, crimes against "people of color" with disabilities, police brutality against disabled Black men, and other topics. Along with advocating for political and institutional change, one of Moore's objectives is to promote understanding. He hopes to see the Black community demonstrate greater unity with its disabled members and learn how to rear its disabled children.

"Parents have to teach African-American disabled children about their culture," said Moore on a recent radio talk show. "We have our own culture, our own music, our own history. A lot of African-American people don't know that this is so." Moore lists heroine Harriet Tubman among the disabled because of the brain injury that led to her seizures and narcolepsy, and he reminds us that the majority of the disabled didn't have the opportunity to escape to freedom with Tubman, because she couldn't take them on her Underground Railroad trips. Umoja requires that in seeking equal access and better lives, we not forget our disabled brothers and sisters. (See www.leroymoore.com.)

❋ Significant efforts are being made to reunite African descendants across the world. The African Diaspora Community has been officially recognized as the Sixth Region of the African Union by its member states. The Western Hemisphere African Diaspora Network (WHADN) was chosen to spread the news. Through the assistance of organizations and individuals in Africa, the United States, and the Caribbean, the organization raised over two million dollars to finance an April 2006 public information tour to four U.S. cities and to Barbados and Jamaica. During the tour, African descendants were asked to complete a questionnaire designed to identify their preferences, level of interest, and readiness to take advantage of the opportunity. A report on the WHADN Web site posed: "What will be the future status of the African Diaspora—status quo, dual citizenship, various African national citizenships, a single African Union or United States of Africa citizenship? These questions are being answered now and the African Diaspora themselves must participate in answering the questions" (www.whadn.org).

In a separate but related event, presidents of twelve African nations met with U.S. business and political leaders at a July 2006 summit in Nigeria. One discussion concerned the securing of African citizenship for the descendants of enslaved Africans. Heading a committee to consider how this could be achieved is Anthony Archer, a Santa Monica, California–based lawyer. Several ideas are on the table to address the issue, considering that most descendants don't know the original homeland of their forebears. But even this is a potentially manageable issue using a DNA test developed by Black scientist Dr. Rick Kittles of African Ancestry, Inc. This simple mail-in cheek-swab test, taken by thousands of clients thus far, can trace ancestral roots back to a region in Africa, and even to a particular village (www.africanancestry.com).

Finally, Atlanta's Emory University will use a $324,000 National Endowment for the Humanities grant to create a Web site featuring the ship logs, manifests, and maps with routes from more than 80 percent of the transatlantic slave trade voyages. The material will be presented for use by scholars with a section devoted to K–12 education and may be useful in the quest to identify places of origin for millions of people of African ancestry.

Kujichagulia 365—Each Day Can Be a Self-Determining One

❋ Be an informed consumer of media. Decide for yourself what to think about things and investigate sources and agendas. Rather than just reading your newspaper alone and discarding it, come together occasionally with others to discuss what's happening in your neighborhood and in the world. Seek out alternative news, be it via print or broadcast. Know the parent companies of those "mainstream" press outlets you do utilize and evaluate any possible bias. Support the Black press, which often publishes articles of importance to our communities and gives a voice to scholars and strategists who can't find column space elsewhere. Keep the Black press alive during a challenging time for the publishing industry by purchasing subscriptions to Black-owned newspapers, magazines, and journals. Contribute to your local listener-supported radio or viewer-supported television station.

❋ Know your history: it's a route to self-esteem and clear thinking. You can make more informed choices about the direction of your own life and the mission of your family or group if you know what came before and how it came to be. Share the historical knowledge you gain with young people and volunteer to organize a study group at a local community venue. If you master a subject, consider writing about it in order to contribute to creating a more balanced view of the historical journey of people of African descent.

❋ Deliberate, dialogue, and soul-search to determine what's in your own best interest and best for your community. Don't be dependent on others for your education on community concerns, but be sure to take advantage of those resources that are in place, such as courses on public policy and world events taught at your local college campus. Acknowledge your right to take a stand for these issues after you've become informed. Work from within your community with those directly affected by the issues. Forming coalitions can be useful, but it is your group's prerogative, and not the only way that a group can be effective.

❋ Think about what you call yourself and how you wish to be referred to and addressed. In your personal life, require mutual respect; if you don't like the way someone addresses you on the street, don't answer. Be aware also that although it may not matter much to you, what Black people are officially called is an important issue to some. In this book, the author consciously refers to people of the African Diaspora in various ways. The term "African-American" identifies my "race" and place of birth, but can distance me from those of my people who were born elsewhere. Many people insist on being identified as "African" with no hyphenation or apology, in order to be identified with the place from which their ancestors originated. If this bothers you, ask yourself if you'd be bothered by a woman born in Chicago who say she's Italian or a man born in Detroit wearing a button that says, "Kiss Me, I'm Irish!" They decline to identify themselves in hyphenated terms, not because they're attempting to hide the obvious, but because they take pride in an ancestral heritage that contributes to the multiple cultures found in the Americas. It's now also useful, in my opinion, to use the term "Black-African" to identify those who are African by lineage among people of European, Asian, or East Indian descent who were born in Africa.

❋ Don't use or condone the "N word." In fact, any term with such a ridiculous nickname is clearly beneath you. We are well versed in the rationales, so there's no need to rehash them, except to say that it's not in keeping with Kujichagulia to embrace or perpetuate a slur against your people. See the pathology in using your prerogative to name yourself to adopt the derogatory names others have called you. For a reality-check anecdote, see www.washingtoninformer.com/OPED editorial-2005Aug18.html, and also, www.rushprnews.com/david-sylvester-contribute2-org-9876543212345678.htm. If you need assistance, see www.abolishthenword.com.

Kujichagulia Works

❋ The East, a Black Nationalist organization based in Brooklyn, New York, opened in 1969 and thrived through the mid-1980s, leaving a legacy influential across the world. It was headed by education and community activist Jitu Weusi and developed from the African American Teachers Association (ATA), which formed in the wake of the Ocean Hill–Brownsville struggle for community control of the schools. When members of the African American Students Association (ASA) were suspended from school for their active support of these efforts, ATA members taught six-hour school sessions each evening to prepare them for the GED. Almost immediately after the opening of its Claver Place base of operations, The East opened Uhuru Sasa school with a handful of students; later that year it would become a full-service educational institution serving preschool, elementary, and high school students.

Throughout its active life, The East embodied the spirit and manifested the objectives of Kujichagulia. The organization opened and successfully ran a bookstore, food cooperative, catering business, restaurant, jazz club, newspaper, clothing store, and daycare center. It launched theatrical productions, supported grassroots political campaigns, established a land development cooperative with the nation of Guyana, and formed alliances with numerous Pan African organizations in the States and abroad. The East also founded the International African Arts Festival (called the African Street Carnival at birth), a world-renowned culture, arts, and economic gathering which celebrated its thirty-sixth anniversary this year. While the formal organization is no more, members still consider themselves The East Family, and they come from all parts of the nation to gather for an annual Kwanzaa celebration, during which small scholarship grants are given via a drawing to their children and grandchildren. Weusi has also kept the spirit of The East and Kujichagulia alive through his community work. He is the chairperson of both the New York City Chapter of the National Black United Front and the Central Brooklyn Jazz Consortium, which helped to bring New Yorkers to South Africa for that nation's first Jazz Africa Heritage Festival in February 2007. Find out more about the Consortium at www.centralbrooklynjazz.org, and read Kwasi Konadu's book on The East published by Africa World Press.

❋ In New York City, several small groups of individuals work together through womanhood rites of passage. Atilah Basile-Ile Kadijah

Odedefaa Manyansa, a longtime initiated priestess of the Eedyi Tradition of Mali and Senegal, has, since 1976, graduated over 125 teens, young, and middle-aged women seeking a stabilizing and affirming experience. The training can take a year or more and no one graduates until everyone in the group is ready. The goal is to help develop women who can form strong, supportive, and committed bonds with other women, be functional adults in the community, and maintain and model our culture and pass it along to the next generation. They learn a host of things that women in traditional African societies knew how to do; a number of these are skills most modern women would love to have in their toolkits.

"The Dyaiseuo [trainees] learn the history of our people at home and abroad, as well as traditional prayers, songs, dances, spiritual principles, how to pour libation, and how to speak some of the language," says Atilah. "They also gain some mastery of beading, sewing, quilting, cooking for all kinds of diets, what goes in a first aid kit, the workings of the female body, how to bring a baby into the world if necessary, and how to change the oil in their cars." These women exemplify Kujichagulia as they voluntarily seek what they need and then persevere through a rigorous though joyful process. For information on the womanhood training, contact iyatala@gmail.com.

❋ M. A. McKenzie knows the value of Kujichagulia and the focus it requires; self-determination helped her survive when she was forced to begin living on her own at a very early age. Realizing that her own hard-won experience was an invaluable reference, McKenzie began working as a counselor for victims of abuse, substance abusers, and the homeless. She distilled the lessons of her journey into a self-published book entitled *The Core of It All: Self Actualization—A Component of Principle.*

A major portion of McKenzie's book is devoted to the Nguzo Saba as a skill-building system. Her theory states that each of the Nguzo Saba can be used as a behavioral change tool. In fact, she inverts the order of the principles for this purpose, positing that faith is the first step in embarking on a journey to actualization and that the destination is unity, where personality and behavior come in line with values and objectives. *The Core of It All* offers insight into self-assessment and journaling, provides daily and weekly exercises, and suggests actions to be taken in order to create tangible progress. (Visit www.xlibris.com.)

❋ If there's one aspect of Kujichagulia with which people of African descent have resonated, it's naming ourselves; many of us have exercised our right to change our name, and most who haven't have respected the right of others to be called whatever they please. We've demonstrated a healthy return to pride in our heritage by naming our children, businesses, and projects after African people, places, and concepts. Along the way, however, some of us lost our bearings when, inspired by African names and attempting to achieve the "unique," we gave our children concocted names with no meaning that later proved to be anything but unique.

Practice informed self-determination by judiciously choosing a name for yourself or for your loved ones. There are many books on the subject and lists on the Internet; do the research and choose names that reflect your values and aspirations. If you are set on creating an "original" name, however, consider the practice of some adherents to Kemetic tradition, who devise words or a phrase that captures the spirit of the journey the person will walk and the virtues to be upheld. Naming is an honor: let's respect it by giving it due consideration. (An interesting look at how the naming issue can affect a community is offered in this account of people naming a middle school in Kansas City, Missouri: see www.nbufront.org/html/BushTelegraph/ACE_SchoolName Contr.html.)

Ujima 365—Consistent Collective Work and Responsibility

❋ Be involved in educating our own: in the home, in the classroom, and in the community. Our ancestors risked their lives to steal a few moments learning to read or write. Imagine how privileged they'd consider us to be, to have the option to openly guide our children to excellence and to open our own schools. Take every opportunity to teach your child about life and to instill the perspective and educational skills needed to prevail. Support independent Black schools: it's a clear win-win scenario. If your child can't attend one exclusively, consider having him or her spend those formative early childhood years at one. If you choose the right environment, it can contribute greatly to producing a young person of pride with a resilient sense of self. Be an active parent at the school by joining the PTA or helping out from home if you can't attend meetings. If you don't have children, consider writing a check to an independent school from time to time or going by to volunteer every once in a while.

❋ View it as partially your problem if the young people in your community aren't getting a good education, even if you don't have children in the schools. Express your concern to local elected officials and publicly at a PTA meeting, in letters to the editor, or by joining with others to organize a press conference. Also speak privately to a neighbor whose children are affected. Find out what you can do to help, whether it's tutoring once a week, helping a teacher buy supplies for her classroom, or mentoring a youth whose parents are uninvolved at school. If you are a parent, get involved at school, as best you can.

❋ Your knowledge of African history, how cars work, or how to build a Web site will fascinate the right child. Ask around or work through a community center to find that child. If you're a great cook, there may be a teen you know who'd love to learn, but whose parents are too busy to teach. Invite her or him to help you make dinner and then have the parents come over to share the meal.

❋ Visit an elder who's living in a nursing home or who doesn't have much family around. He or she may not be your relative but will greatly appreciate and look forward to a little company now and then. Even if you're too busy, find the time. Encourage your children to come along or, if they're old enough, to visit elders on their own. This helps send the message that your family is serious in regards to "our brothers' and sisters' problems." It takes only a small sacrifice of time to address the big problem of loneliness.

❋ Pick up the slack for someone in an emergency, someone who may be grieving or in shock. Oftentimes we're not sure what to say or do when life intensely impacts those around us. Be observant to see what needs doing and move quickly. You might offer to run some errands, pick a child up from school, or make phone calls for someone who's simply unable.

❋ Pick up trash in your neighborhood. You don't have to be a one-person sanitation route, but if you see junk advertising circulars you know your neighbor doesn't want in front of her house, scoop them up. Your consistent example will inspire others to do more to help maintain the community.

❋ Don't allow anyone to be abused without your speaking up or making the necessary notifications. *It is your business* if a young person is sexually threatened or harmed, if a woman is beaten by her partner, if someone has a brutal encounter with law enforcement, if a child is bullied in your neighborhood or enslaved in The Sudan. See it as your responsibility to intervene in a way that does not place you or your family in danger. Investigate the options, summon the courage, and don't wait until it's too late.

❋ Consider opening your family to a child if you can make room in your life, heart, and home. Media reports still speak of the high number of "unwanted children" of African descent languishing in foster care. The world has adopted the African proverb "It takes a village to raise a child." Surely these children of our village are not unwanted. If you aren't in a position to adopt a child, perhaps you can volunteer some time to a foster care agency so that the children there will know there are people who care.

Ujima Works

❋ Education is an arena in which Ujima is critical; Nazalima Stephanie Durham knows this firsthand. She's worked in the New York City school system for nineteen years, in the classroom, as a multicultural specialist, literacy coach, teacher trainer, enrichment supervisor, and in other capacities. She's known for her love of children, rapport with parents, and seemingly inexhaustible supply of ideas for keeping everyone engaged and on the same page. But she's the first to say that help is needed.

"I think schools have to have parents as partners and partnerships with the community, as well," Durham says. "The way education is going, our children need to learn from all areas. We need more people who are willing to help provide programming and activities, knowledge-based programs where their hobbies, skills, or talents are invaluable in the classroom."

Durham has organized things such as movie nights at school for parents and their children, and cabaret-style poetry slams with dimmed lights, candles on the lunchroom tables, and kids serving as waiters. She also trained and organized students to run a profitable on-site bookstore at her elementary school. Whatever the material to be learned, Durham finds that students respond and retain best when fun and new experiences are incorporated. She'd like to see community members play more of a role in making this happen.

"Each child needs to feel that the adults in the world care, are responsible for them, and that they can be safe," says Durham. "That is the unseen benefit of people working together." See Chapter 9, "Kwanzaa Resources," for Durham's suggestions of some great books for our children.

❋ The Grassroots Steering Foundation Inc. (GRSF), based in Baltimore, Maryland, is an example of Ujima in action. Since its founding in 1997, GRSF members, rather than sitting back shaking their heads, have gotten involved to help alleged victims of unfair treatment or abuse in encounters with law enforcement in the tristate area of Maryland, Washington D.C., and Virginia. Foundation members conduct seminars, aid clients in filing complaints, schedule and attend meetings with authorities and community leaders, and refer attorneys. They investigate incidents, serve as spokespersons when legally permissible, and find that the respecting of basic rights is an issue for African Americans across socioeconomic categories (www.steeringfoundation.org/4436.html).

❋ Adeyemi Bandele, a resident of Baltimore, Maryland, is a Lincoln University professor and founder and executive director of Men on the Move, "a spirit-based men's empowerment movement." The organization created A Gathering of Men, a network of support groups which has, since 1999, met in Washington D.C., Phoenix, Atlanta, Detroit, New York, and other cities, and in places such as Bermuda and Brazil. The men are showing up to support one another in the work of unmasking, healing, and growing. Bandele says the intergenerational setting helps the group to accomplish significant work.

"Men on the Move is designed to empower men to stand in their truth as better fathers, sons, husbands, lovers, and friends," says Bandele. "We come together to heal and to celebrate these relationships. A lot of us have grown up with our fathers absent or missing, some have passed away. Men are missing their relationships and families and sometimes they also miss brothers and friends who are no longer in their lives. People come, work through their anger, resentment, and grief, and leave with tools to address their trauma. Along with the healing we also make it a point to celebrate healthy, wholesome relationships."

MOM has also established and coordinates A Gathering of the Family, which helps participants to evaluate the impact of the mate relationship in the intact family. "Fathers and Sons: A Celebration and Healing" is a process designed to aid in the repair and strengthening of that relationship. Clearly, the organization is actively contributing to getting men of African descent focused on Ujima. To contact Men on the Move, call (240) 432-6081 or e-mail adeyummi@aol.com.

❋ Bandele's son Lumumba is proof that commitment to community work often passes on to our children. A resident of his native Brooklyn, New York, Lumumba Bandele was raised by his father and his mother, Khadija, to be a responsive and contributing member of society. He is national co-coordinator of The Malcolm X Grassroots Movement (MXGM), founded by his wife, Monifa Akinwole Bandele. Lumumba's work has always involved initiatives to inform and unite the people. He found his counterpart in Monifa, a visionary young activist with the courage of her convictions and then some. The MXGM, with chapters in six cities, has served over 4,000 meals to the homeless in Central Brooklyn, provided them with recycled clothing, and helped them to organize around their human rights. Their Central Brooklyn Cop Watch program established patrols aimed at preventing and documenting the use of brutal force, and its Political Prisoner Amnesty Campaign has organized mass mobilizations to bring attention to the plight of the injustices faced by people such as Geronimo Jijaga Pratt, whose conviction was overturned after he'd spent twenty-seven years in prison.

"The Malcolm X Grassroots Movement spearheaded Katrina on the Ground, which sent over 2,000 students to the Gulf region in the aftermath of the hurricane," says Lumumba. "They worked in demolition and construction, counseling and training."

Lumumba is also the cofounder of the Black August Hip Hop Project, which has helped to bridge gaps among communities across the world where Hip Hop culture is prominent. The organization is inspired by the month-long observance founded in 1970 by prisoners in the California penal system. It involved fasting, study, and political education. Black August sponsors youth education and empowerment conferences and has taken young people to Cuba, Brazil, South Africa, and Tanzania, trips financed in part by its annual benefit concert, which has featured headliners such as Erykah Badu, The Roots, and Talib Kweli. The organization's mission states: "Our goal is to bring culture and politics together and to allow them to naturally evolve into a unique Hip Hop consciousness that informs our collective struggle for a more just and equitable world." See www.mxgm.org and www.blackaugust.com.

❋ There are many unsung community heroes who share their skills with our youth, embodying Ujima by equipping our youth with skills to earn an independent living. Anu Prestonia of New York City's Khamit Kinks hair salon is one of these. She started out working alone and on a small scale, braiding, twisting, and doing other inventive things with Black women's hair. Her fine work and professionalism soon led to a few high-profile clients and work as a stylist across the nation. When she was in a position to open her first shop, she made sure to involve several teenage girls in her community—a win-win situation and more.

"I taught them the foundational basics," Anu says, "such as how to execute professional braiding techniques and efficient ways to work. They had assignments each week with mannequin heads so that I could see their progress, and those who progressed well were offered positions at the salon. I later helped several of them to go into business for themselves, and all who've left the salon remain successfully self-employed."

As the girls became young women, they were there to witness the growth of a business that remains attentive to community needs. Khamit Kinks created Casamance Braids in tribute to the Senegalese city of that name, put Goddess Braids on the map after doing Queen Latifah's hair, and served as stylists for several *Essence* magazine beauty features. Angela Bassett, Suzanne Douglass, and Terry McMillan are sometime clients, Anu has done Oprah's hair, and Stevie Wonder is a loyal client who comes in when he's on the East Coast. The shop has hosted AIDS awareness, domestic-abuse awareness, and other events, and Anu, also a certified yoga instructor, has taught a free women's yoga class in Brooklyn. She hopes the young women who continue to come to work at Khamit Kinks are inspired to be of service and that they also have an informed view of what it takes to make it.

Ujamaa 365—Cooperative Economics Every Day

❋ The first order of business in bringing cooperative economics to life is to feel good about investing your money in businesses owned by people of African descent. You are acting responsibly in doing what all other successful people do: helping your own rather than waiting for someone else to do it.

❋ Become educated about finances. In the United States, where the Black dollar fails to circulate even once before leaving the community, Black households collectively earned $679 billion in the year 2004 (www.targetmarketnews.com/BuyingPower05.htm). These staggering resources, if invested in our communities, could eliminate substandard housing, unemployment, and inadequate health care among other ills.

Opening an account at a Black bank is one simple thing you can do. If none are in your area, try OneUnited, the first Black-owned financial institution to offer online banking (www.one united.com).

❋ Get in the habit of planning ahead to determine which goods and services you can obtain from Black-owned businesses without undue hardship. Prepare for any time this may add to your regular routine and seek solutions; in some cases, you may even find that you save time. Get your entire household on board and acknowledge the satisfaction of knowing that your money, rather than just going down the proverbial drain, is being put to important use. Make conscious decisions in other situations, as well. For example, book a group reservation at a Black-owned restaurant for the office Kwanzaa luncheon rather than running over to the usual spot.

❋ Graciously require responsive, top-notch service: if you don't, you'll become frustrated and abandon your efforts prematurely. We all know our people are capable of giving 110% when necessary. If you're not satisfied, let the business owner know, in a respectful way, that your support is deliberate and that you'll refer others when you see improvement. If there's no improvement, move on without bitterness to an alternative business.

❋ Join a buying club or food cooperative to get more for your money and patronize the local Black farmers' market (www.mobetterfood.com). If these options aren't available in your community, join with others to create them. Become part of a savings, investment, or other Black-wealth-building group. Share your financial expertise if you have it and invest, if you can, in someone's dream to open a business or purchase property. If you've been blessed, consider giving a small scholarship, perhaps in a relative's name, to a Black student in need.

❋ Refuse to support businesses or industries that disrespect you, misrepresent your interests, or take your patronage for granted, be they Black-owned or other. Don't finance misogyny, criminality, buffoonery, or depravity and then wonder why things aren't better.

❋ Don't try to buy self-esteem—it's not for sale. No amount of bling, arm candy or auto candy, overpriced clothes, or high-roller gift-giving will compensate for the damage done to a people told they weren't valuable or beautiful enough just as God made them. Some of us have had additional injury inflicted by abusive or incompetent parents. If you need therapy, spend some money on that, and if you can't afford it, join a support group or buy self-help books before allowing debt to ruin you.

❋ Don't listen to people who say that Ujamaa is an idea whose time has come and gone. They wouldn't go to Chinatown or to a Hasidic neighborhood, for example, and tell the residents that patronizing one another's businesses is passé. Neither do they offer proven alternatives for achieving the quality of self-sufficiency that these communities enjoy.

❋ Feel a sense of urgency. In many areas our children cannot find employment where they live or, as they grow older, rent an apartment in the neighborhood in which they were raised. Refuse to contribute to the marginalization of your people through willful ignorance of the effects of your economic decisions.

❋ Don't hate. Not your friend for having more, yourself for not having enough, your neighbor for having less. Don't resent Oprah, even if you disagree with how she chooses to use her formidable wealth and clout. (See "We Still Wear the Mask" at www.jelanicobb.com/port folio.html, and "Oprah's Good Intentions" at www.blackagenda report.com for two views on the subject.) Hate is poisonous, envy debilitating, and resentment nonproductive. Love instead. Love your potential to advance; love your friend for encouraging you, your family for supporting you, and your community for investing in you. And if you happen to be employed by a Black-owned business, give it that 110%.

❋ If you are a business owner, broaden your reach. Research the many opportunities available to do business with other people of African descent, be they suppliers, distributors, or service providers doing business in East Africa, England, or around the corner from your house.

Ujamaa Works

❋ Karibu Books opened with $500 in 1993 as a street-vending business in Washington, D.C. Today it is a chain of six stores, including those in Arlington, Virginia, and Baltimore, Maryland. It carries over 8,000 titles and hosts over 600 authors a year (karibubooks.com).

❋ In New York City, Nubian Heritage started on the street as well, selling incense and oils in downtown Brooklyn in 1992. By 2004, it was doing business as a major distributor of its own line of natural body care products and had grown to such proportions that it was able to come to the rescue of the National Black Theater, which due to rising gentrification, was priced out of its decades-long Harlem base. Nubian Heritage purchased the building, now valued at over $14 million. It serves as home to the company's flagship store, the Theater was able to remain, and stores such as The Body Shop are tenants (www.nubianheritage.com).

❋ The International African Arts Festival started as a block-party fundraiser with vendors' tables in Brooklyn, New York. Thirty-six years later, it has grown into a five-day event with attendees, performers, and merchants coming faithfully each year from across the country, from Africa, and from the Caribbean. Chief of Operations Mzee Moyo says the community patronizes more than 250 vendors and that money circulates more than once around the Festival to other vendors. Merchants have used their earnings to pay college tuition or to make the down payment on a storefront. A few nationally known businesses, including the natural toiletries company Carol's Daughter and designer clothing line Moshood, were Festival merchants in their infancy (www.iaafestival.org).

❋ The African Peoples Farmers Market, also in Brooklyn, was born as a once-weekly outdoor enterprise reselling quality produce purchased at the terminal market to neighbors at fair prices. It was organized by the Harriet Tubman–Fannie Lou Hamer Collective in response to the continuing disrespect consumers felt they were shown by Korean merchants nearly a decade after a proprietor was accused of assaulting a customer in 1990, leading to a seventeen-month boycott of the store. The Market operated on a Bedford-Stuyvesant street corner for seven years before moving into a storefront in 1996 and opening Sistas' Place, a well-respected jazz club and community meeting/organizing space (www.sistasplace.org).

❋ Walter Mosley stunned the publishing world in 1997 when, in the midst of blockbuster success, he allowed tiny Black Classic Press to reap the financial rewards of publishing *Gone Fishin'*, the next novel in his Easy Rawlins mystery series. He said he did it to challenge other successful African Americans to do likewise and has since published *What Next: A Memoir Toward World Peace* with Black Classic as well. Mosley had been preceded decades earlier by Pulitzer Prize–winning poet Gwendolyn Brooks, who, having just published her most commercially successful book, turned to Dudley Randall's tiny, Black-owned Broadside Press to publish her next work and then reinvested her royalties back into his company. She would later publish with Haki Madhubuti's Third World Press as well (www.blackclassic.com).

❋ Recently, Tavis Smiley, an author and television and radio host, collaborated with prolific writer and vocal Princeton University professor Cornel West, on a book entitled *The Covenant with Black America*, which offers a treatise and 10-point action plan for the problems African Americans face. Smiley had intended before starting the book to go with a Black publisher, and he chose Third World Press. Due to Smiley's reach as an on-air personality, West's high public profile, and a nationwide "town hall meeting" tour, *The Covenant* placed at No. 1 on Amazon.com and on the Barnes & Noble and Borders lists and No. 6 on the *New York Times* bestseller list. The book is paying off for the authors, for their highly appreciative publishing company, and for readers, who are well served by a concrete example of Ujamaa (www.third

worldpressinc.com). A critical take on the tour is at www.afro-netizen.com/2006/03/talented_tenth_.html.

❋ Cooperative economics requires that we reflect on our consumer activity. In July 2005, Yankelovich, Inc., declared that the buying habits of African Americans could be predicted by their position in one of six segments—emulators, seekers, reachers, attainers, conservers, and elites. However, in stating her reaction to this study, McGhee Williams Osse, co-CEO of Burrell Communications, a veteran Black-owned advertising agency, insists that Black identity plays a larger role.

"Despite these segment differences, there is still a strong racial awareness that has resulted in Black pride and a deep solidarity with other African Americans, which affects purchasing decisions," says Williams Osse. "African Americans say they are loyal to companies that reflect an understanding of this awareness and their ethnic affinity. Non-Hispanic white marketers, who have not experienced exclusion based on race or color, may find it difficult to understand that this sensitivity exists, particularly since it is a feeling that is shared by African Americans across the board, even at the highest social strata and economic brackets" (www.yankelovich.com/media/MMSReleaseFinal.pdf).

Nia 365—The Power of a Purpose-Driven Year

❋ Discuss what your family stands for and the legacy it will leave. Then come up with a family objective, a mission statement that represents it, and a strategy for achieving it. Identify things you value in common and the marching orders you received from your forebears.

Is your family known for initiating improvements to the neighborhood, becoming active in local politics, delivering food to homeless shelters, or nurturing young artists? If no one in your household has an interest in politics and everyone's too busy for neighborhood projects, consider alternative ways of making that traditional contribution, perhaps by writing a check or getting your company to donate materials or provide sponsorship.

❋ Take things personally, speak up when asked, and demonstrate your care for the well-being of others. Lend your voice to those in need or to those who will use it to help better societal conditions. If you're secure in a well-paying job, you can still call your congressman about increasing the minimum wage. If you're not losing sleep over the scarcity of affordable housing, you can still make your voice heard on behalf of the working poor. Although you may not have children, you can mentor a teen who's wrestling with life decisions and won't talk to a parent, but will open up to another concerned adult. In the process you may find the opportunity to steer that young person back to the bosom of family, if that's a healthy choice.

❋ Teach your children to practice Nia by sharing their time, talents, and resources with others; the recipients will benefit, and you'll produce a young person with healthier self-esteem. Encourage them to do what they can as young individuals to contribute to the vitality of their community. Show them the inspiring news stories of young people who have done just that. Help them to organize their friends or classmates into a small group that can make a big difference. Remind them also that the greatest reward comes not from public recognition, but from knowing that their labor on behalf of others will bear fruit.

❋ Actively counter the messages that devalue our worth. If cable television and billboard ads are presenting images of crassly materialistic or self-devaluing Black people, stop watching those channels and buying those products. Clip articles about serious, gifted, and generous people of African descent and display them on your refrigerator, where your kids can't miss them. If the perpetuation of light-skin preference within the Black community concerns you, act to deprogram this response in your own environment. Display a photo or painting of a very dark person in a beautiful frame in a prominent place in your home. Seeing it there each day, your children will feel that the skin that proclaims their ancestry not only is okay, but is a valued source of pride.

❋ Call your local TV news station if all its expert sources come from a homogenous pool. Point them in the direction of a few Black people or organizations that can provide the same information. If you notice that there's a consistently all-white roster of winners for a local youth competition, contact the organizers and inquire about their efforts to publicize the contest in Black communities.

❋ Support independent Black institutions of all types. Go to see the plays at the neighborhood theater, donate to the program that helps teenage girls develop self-esteem or one that mentors teen fathers. Lend your skills to an organization teaching the elderly to use the Internet, or go talk to students at a local independent school on career day. Seek out people working on projects or issues that interest you. It may be an environmental group or one that aids ailing retired entertainers. The point is to make your convictions stand for something in the world.

Nia Works

❋ When The Ontario Black History Society, headed by Dr. Rosemary Sadlier, began working to establish Kwanzaa in Canada, its efforts were informed by previous successes. In 1979 it declared February as Black History Month in Toronto and campaigned for seventeen years for its national recognition. The organization also founded Emancipation Day, celebrated on August 1, with national status pending. Interestingly, however, the Society will not push to have Kwanzaa declared an official national observance.

"The OBHS opted not to take it further," says Sadlier, "since the pure, value-based nature of the celebration was quickly being seized upon as the 'Black Christmas,' with all the commercialism that entails. To keep it true, we've left it at the city level and we do put on a ceremony. Others within the African-Canadian community do so as well."

❋ Baba Kwame Ishangi was beloved across the United States and in parts of the Caribbean, Africa, and Europe as a passionate keeper of culture. A 1980 World Peace Medalist, Ishangi was a phenomenal dancer and folklorist who lived and breathed all things creatively and spiritually African. His Ishangi Family African Dancers amazed and enlightened audiences far and wide. Baba was known also for constructing beautiful ancestral altars at events such as Brooklyn Academy of Music's annual "Dance Africa!" festival. For a decade before his untimely death in 2003, he made time between cultural appearances and his work as a priest to focus on the establishing of his lifelong dream-come-true, Ishangi Kunda, a haven built on land in the Gambia, West Africa, village of Tanji that would serve as a shrine to the ancestors of the middle passage and be visited by people of African descent the world over.

He dreamed of a place with comfortable traditional accommodations where people could gather to worship, hold conferences and symposiums, and present cultural entertainment. He stayed on purpose, talking about it constantly, never allowing the vision to fade until it was brought to life not long before his passing.

The Ishangi family rallied with the help of friends and longtime supporters and kept his dreams alive. The dance company still travels and performs, with the younger generation now in charge. The Ishangi Kunda stands tucked away on grounds flush with vegetable and herb gardens and newly planted mango, avocado, cashew, lime, and papaya trees. The main house has hosted several groups and conferences, and the little round houses have served as lodging for many visitors making their first pilgrimage to the land of their forebears. The Ishangi family demonstrates that in uniting around a purpose we can ensure that it prevails and transcends beyond its source. For information on Ishangi Kunda, contact Akua N. Ishangi at (718) 873-4449, visit www.ishangi.com/kunda, or e-mail info@ishangi.com. To contact the Ishangi Family African Dancers, call (703) 764-0180.

❋ Inspired by the Nguzo Saba, *On Nia* is an action-planning tool for adults and young adults who are seeking to make successful life transitions. It was devised by African Heritage Academy founder Louis Young (see Chapter 3). Through popular response, it evolved from a pamphlet workbook to a weekly column in *The City Sun*, a defunct Black newspaper that served the New York metro area in the 1980s and 1990s.

"*On Nia* is a reminder that Africans should live life on purpose, with a meaningful end in mind," says Young. "We remain aware of our values and choose the means by which we'll live in harmony with those values." The following is one of five suggestions offered in an *On Nia* column entitled "Brain Ase" (Brain Power). It is used with the permission of the author as one example of how we can think "on purpose."

> *Use all seven of your "brains" to learn. Mainstream education works with only two aspects of your intelligence: the linguistic and the mathematical-logical. To release your Imhotepean (multifaceted) potential, you should tap your other five intelligences: visual-spatial, musical, bodily-kinesthetic, interpersonal and intrapersonal. By applying all of these seven to your learning, you'll accelerate your learning power."*

Find out more at www.africanheritageacademy.com or contact duboismalcolm@hotmail.com.

❋ Michael Hooper is the founder and director of Roots Revisited, a cultural literacy program servicing youth based in Brooklyn, New York. The group takes youth on tours of Black college campuses, on local trips to museums, libraries, galleries, and historic sites such as the African Burial Ground, Seneca Village, and the homes of Harriet Tubman and Frederick Douglass. Some participants are aided in finding summer employment and in obtaining community service positions that can earn them up to six independent-study credits. The annual trips to Africa, however, are the soul of the program. Hooper and his staff have taken high school and college students to twenty-three African nations, including Benin, Malawi, Cameroon, Zimbabwe, Ethiopia, Ghana, and Nigeria. Youth with technology skills have helped to set up Internet cafés, and others have hefted bricks and drywall to help build two schools and a library in Tanzania.

"We've been in conversation with Black engineers about training a contingent of youth and adults to assemble solar power systems," says Hooper. "This group will then travel to villages in Africa where there's no electricity or running water and train students there, who'll then be able to work together to bring solar power to one another's homes."

The programs at Roots Revisited are largely self-supported through donations, the selling of raffle tickets, and fundraising events, because Hooper says that grants, while welcome, often come little and late. A Nia consciousness and a strong determination to make a difference are the capital and the energy source that keep Roots Revisited going. Roots is always open to people who want to lend a hand. Contact them at www.rootsrevisited.org or at (718) 773-0246.

Kuumba 365—Creativity as a Year-Round Focus

❋ If you're an artist of any kind, take yourself seriously. Study those whom you admire while safeguarding your own style. Set aside time to practice your craft, and once it's scheduled, don't cancel it unless an emergency arises. Let your children see you making time to be an artist. Don't be discouraged if people find your new habits strange or even amusing; they're not used to seeing you in this light. Be consistent and they'll get used to it. Join a writers' group or artists' collective to get and give support.

❋ Have something to say. Work to make your art fulfilling for you and for its intended consumers. Don't be afraid to be an outspoken or risk-taking artist, but also remain aware of the powerful effects of your medium. In many traditional African societies, artists went through ini-

tiation rites. Because these art-makers worked with sound, imagery, and other powerfully influential media, the society took an interest in their level of consciousness and in the establishing of their values. Talk to a mentor or be your own elder and honestly consider not only your aesthetics, but your artistic ethics.

❋ Support those artists who make a conscious decision to create work that strengthens and inspires the community, be they filmmakers, or recording or visual artists. Consciously spend your money on their products, sending a message to the entertainment industry about what you value and would like to see or hear more often. Spread the word to your friends and your e-mail contacts when you've found a positive artist you enjoy. Go out to see that artist in person if he or she makes a public appearance in your area.

❋ Place your art at the service of the community. Work on a mural, design a costume, help write a song for the school play, or volunteer to teach a crafts workshop at a senior center or daycare facility. Teach a young person how to write, draw, sew, do computer graphic design, or produce a radio show.

❋ Try something new. Take a dance, photography, or music history class, learn how to speak a new language or play a musical instrument. Sit in on an acting class and then see a play at a regional theater. Dress differently, try a foreign cuisine, see a movie you normally wouldn't, then write a review and e-mail it to friends. Go to a local store to listen to music from other parts of the world and buy some to take home if you can.

❋ Think creatively. When stuck, grab pen and paper and brainstorm at least three different approaches to solving the problem you're experiencing. Research a career field that's always intrigued you and see if you'd be interested in apprenticing in your spare time. Learn about mind-mapping (www.mind-mapping.co.uk/index.htm) and use it to create a blueprint for realizing a dream.

❋ Nurture your child's creativity. Some items you'd normally throw out are the basis for a great craft project; just look at them differently. Give art supplies for birthday and Kwanzaa gifts. Use music and dance to teach basic and even advanced concepts. See free music and dance concerts and visit museums on discount days. If you know a budding photographer, take her out for a day of shooting. Lend a responsible teen your video camera to make a short film. Notice what your child likes to do and support that.

❋ Don't let others decide what you like. For example, a 2006 survey by Fleishman-Hillard Inc. found that 82 percent of African-American women ages twenty-four to forty-nine prefer R&B or soul music to other genres. Yet these artists struggle to get airplay in a market saturated by mediocre hip hop. Entertainment media tell us this is what everybody's listening to, while music distribution companies benefit from the misconception (www.eurweb.com/story/eur27227.cfm).

❋ Educate yourself about your art form. Know the history of your medium and those who've made the greatest impact. If you're a visual artist, know Augusta Savage and Romare Bearden. If you're a DJ, be one of the serious ones with a wealth of knowledge and eclectic taste. If you study dance, know not just Alvin Ailey, but Pearl Primus as well. If you're a poet, study poetry, not just "spoken word." Read Louis Rivera's "Inside the River of Poetry" (www.inmotionmagazine.com/ac/rivera.html) and Kalamu ya Salaam's article on the Black Arts Movement (aalbc.com/authors/blackartsmovement.htm) as well as books on the subject listed in our Kwanzaa Resources, Chapter 9.

❋ Go out to hear live jazz when you can. This art, originated by people of African ancestry and called Black Classical Music by some, is revered the world over, yet club audiences are overwhelmingly white. This is, of course, a financial issue as well, as the complexion ratio changes at free outdoor concerts, and surveys show African Americans listen to jazz at home in greater numbers. However, unlike their parents, who grew up listening to whatever was played in the home, most teens listen exclusively to popular music on their iPods or on cable TV. While there are some exceptions, most don't hear jazz, so they're not fans, enrollment in jazz education programs is disproportionately white, and we're losing our jazz players. Champion jazz at home and find other ways to promote this phenomenal product of our Kuumba.

Kuumba Works

❋ Laurie Cumbo is the founder and director of MoCADA, the Museum of Contemporary African Diasporan Arts in Brooklyn, New York. Her tireless commitment is Kuumba in action and she'd like to see more people appreciate the many gifts the arts have to offer. She starts many museum tours by quoting Franz Fanon: "When you destroy a culture, you destroy a people." She feels that art, history, and culture are the missing elements to making us whole once again.

"Our community needs to get into the habit of supporting cultural institutions the way they do religious institutions because culture is also a way of feeding your spirit. People need to get into the habit of making a contribution on a regular basis and at the very least, get out of the habit of being ashamed of coming in and giving a dollar, or even fifty cents—believe me, the institution will be happy to get it!" (MoCADA.org).

❋ Zahmu Sankofa of Philadelphia uses Kuumba to teach Black history and culture. In 1990 he wrote and released the song "It's Kwanzaa Time," set to a danceable urban contemporary beat. "I basically wanted to help people to say the words correctly and have the meanings stick with them," he recalls. Before he knew it, the song received some airplay and people from across the nation were calling for copies. Teachers were relieved to have an entertaining tool for teaching about Kwanzaa, and Zahmu was bombarded with requests for public appearances.

On the flip side of the cassette was a song entitled "More Than a Month," about Black history. It started another flurry of interest and requests. Zahmu and his group, Three, have performed the song countless times across the country, and the Philadelphia school system has incorporated it into its Black History Month curriculum. "What's really amazing for me is to see people singing along with me at concerts," Zahmu says. "Parents tell me that their kids grew up listening to 'It's Kwanzaa Time' and I was able to perform it for Dr. Karenga at the thirty-fifth anniversary Kwanzaa program in New York City" (morethanamonth.com).

❋ Celebrated as a visual artist, arts activist, and author, Danny Simmons is owner of the Corridor Gallery and sits on the board of the Brooklyn Academy of Music. He is vice president of the New York City–based Rush Philanthropic Arts Foundation, which he cofounded along with his brothers, self-made mogul Russell Simmons and Rev. Joseph Simmons (formerly "Run" of the hip hop group Run-DMC).

Danny sees the Foundation's mission of nurturing creativity as a critical one.

"We need to reach our children and allow them to think outside the box," he says. "They need exposure to things that can get that creative process sparked; once it's started, it spreads to their thinking, their business and social sense . . . their entire approach to life. Our kids are locked out of so many things. The arts are a way to open those doors and get around those barriers" (www.rushphilanthropic.org).

❋ The Moving Form performance ensemble revels in exploring the rich territories of Kuumba. The "co-conspirators," as they call themselves, came together in the late 1980s to create a group in which each member would create live art from his discipline. During performances, poet Will Halsey reads original work as well as classics by Henry Dumas, Robert Hayden, Gwendolyn Brooks, Langston Hughes, and others. Saxophonist Andrew Lamb tells the story through original compositions and improvisation in what the group calls "The Music" (jazz). Artist Jimmy James Greene paints and sketches onstage, rendering his impressions of the poetic and musical concoction. A bassist and drummer sit in regularly, and for years the group was backed by the late and legendary percussionist Andre Strobert, with whom they recorded *The Year of the Endless Moment* (www.engine-studios.com/Store/Release Index.html, click on #27).

❋ Black women haven't historically had much say in how they've been depicted in film, and a host of obstacles often arises when they seek to make the films themselves, including racism, sexism, nepotism, and lack of capital. Carolyn Butts wanted to support those who'd persevered and those struggling to get a toe in the door. She approached her alma mater, Long Island University, Brooklyn Campus, about partnering with her. Ten years later, the Reel Sisters of the Diaspora Film Festival and Lecture Series has screened hundreds of films, presented iconic film industry figures as panelists, hosted award ceremonies, and given cash prizes in a screenwriting competition.

"Women get less than 1 percent of the directing jobs in Hollywood," said Butts. "They don't have access to tell our stories. I thought it would be a powerful thing to get people together to see the work that is getting done." The glowing faces of young female moviemakers who've just sat listening to feedback on their film or advice from legendary filmmaker Julie Dash, for example, reveal that Butts's Kuumba venture was the right idea (www.reelsisters.org).

Imani 365—Keeping the Faith

❋ Be a visionary. See potential when you look at your family members, colleagues, and friends, rather than defining them by their circumstances. Scientists have conclusively determined that thoughts are things. The assessment you hold of others' prospects filters to them in subtle ways without your saying a word. If you must say a word, make it an encouraging one.

❋ Honestly examine your own thoughts. Have you fallen prey to doubts about our prospects as a people or been deflated by those who focus on setbacks rather than achievement? Do you doubt your own ability to change your circumstances or meet a goal? If so, make a conscious effort to restore your faith. Visit someone you've always admired, read an Ida B. Wells biography, and remind yourself of your, and our, previous successes. Use affirmations if needed.

❋ Never say, "That's just like Black people . . ." or worse. In fact, that statement sounds like something a racist would say. African descendants are as infinitely diverse as we are talented. That dismissive statement is inaccurate and insidiously damaging, like the worm in the apple. It's a remnant of the self-hatred sold to us in an attempt to make us better slaves. If you're in the habit of thinking and speaking this way, be especially careful of what you say in front of children, while you work on getting better. For help, read Dr. Joy Leary (www.posttraumaticslavesyndrome.com/drleary) and *Don't Believe the Hype,* by Farai Chideya (www.africanbookstore.net/proddetail.asp?prod=NF1086).

❋ Demonstrate your faith in others. Purchase a college textbook for a relative returning to school or help a friend with a business plan. Make things easier for a family member who's working on a big project by taking on one of their usual tasks. Help someone to organize a showing of their art or plan a showcase for their music. Give to a Black charity that helps people to become self-sufficient.

❋ Go out on a limb. Faith is just a word until you act on it. Force yourself to take the next step on a project or in your life. Summon the courage to change careers or residences. Develop enough emotional courage to love someone. Remove damaging people from your life and have faith that you'll make it without them. Learn about and be on the lookout for self-sabotage, which is usually subtle and almost always originating in fear. Have enough faith in yourself to notice the fear and to pursue your dreams anyway.

❋ Broaden your view of faith. Not everyone believes what you do or worships as you do. Someone may not be affiliated with any religious faith—this doesn't mean they don't have faith. Don't allow others to demonize the faith heritage of your people, and don't do it yourself. Try to comprehend unfamiliar ways of viewing life. Go to the library, surf the Internet, rent videos, and ask questions. You'll find beautiful, moving, and highly spiritual messages in the sacred texts of most traditions. Look for commonalities, usually found in the moral directives for interacting with one another.

Imani Works

❋ Harriet Tubman, alias Moses, alias "The General," exemplified several of the Nguzo Saba; certainly faith was chief among them. Not only were her actions incredibly courageous and her commitment rock-solid, but Tubman's faith was unshakable. Those who knew her remarked on her spiritual intensity. Not everyone knows that Harriet suffered from narcolepsy, a disorder that causes the afflicted to fall into a deep sleep, on the spot and without notice. Imagine the faith that must be summoned to lead a group of fugitive slaves through the dead of night knowing you'd fall asleep along the way, but not knowing when or where. Once you'd reached your destination without being captured and killed, imagine the faith it took to go back to get more slaves—to go back *nineteen times!* That's the Imani gold standard!

❋ St. Paul Community Baptist Church is a vibrant example of the difference a faith community can make in the larger society. Pastor Johnny Ray Youngblood's congregation has built 2,900 homes through his East Brooklyn Congregations Nehemiah Project, and boasts a list of accomplishments too dense to detail here. The church has, since 1994, contributed something uniquely valuable to its members, to the surrounding community, and to people of all faiths nationwide—*The Maafa*

Suite. Conceived as a "staged psychodrama" and first presented in 1994, *The Maafa Suite* brings the Middle Passage to life in song, dance, spectacle, and pathos, offering African descendents a rare opportunity to fully process the magnitude and impact of this devastating crime.

The Maafa Suite is a harrowing but healing journey that audiences take, and the production has grown so popular it's been seen by tens of thousands. People travel from across the United States and have come from the Caribbean and the Virgin Islands. The demand has been so great that the *Maafa* cast has gone on the road to bring the production to congregations in several states. In the last several years the Commemoration of the Maafa has developed into a week-long observance featuring activities for youth and seniors, a pilgrimage to the river, crafts workshops, a tour of the Maafa Museum at the church, and a conference with lectures and workshops to help participants better grasp the history and significance of the transatlantic slave trade and related topics. Randall Robinson, Cornel West, Joy Leary, and many other learned scholars and activists have participated as speakers. The *Maafa* organizers say it's had a profound therapeutic and unifying effect.

"To say it's an eye-opener is an understatement," says Clay Fielding, executive coordinator for *The Maafa.* "It's an impacting piece, even as you're going through the work. Everyone, from the guest presenters to the cast, is affected as we prepare. People who've seen it say they've been inspired to trace their family history and to heal rifts in the family. That is why the church does it—so many things can be addressed through it and we are blessed that it is so successful." *The Maafa Suite* is held the third week of September each year, and a new addition, "The Maafa: The Struggle Continues," now runs each February. See *www.themaafa.com* for information and touring venues.

❋ Sometimes opportunities arise to examine our ideas around the subject of faith. At a wedding reception, the bride's family members, many of whom are Christian, were brought together with family and friends of the groom, many of whom are not. At one point the groom's mother announced that the time had come to observe an old African ritual. There were a few squirms of discomfort and some cool stares. She then asked if elders present would share words of wisdom with the newlyweds. That was it. Moments later, a friend of the groom's family asked everyone to observe as the couple took part in a traditional African ritual. Again ripples of trepidation. The groom's mother held a plate with small amounts of things for the couple to taste: honey, representing the sweet times; lemon, because life is sometimes sour; pepper, to keep things hot and spicy; and a few more. That was it.

If you would have been uneasy at this reception, ask yourself why. Catholics have a ritual they call "eating the body of the Christ," practicing Jews eat only unleavened bread during Passover, and Christmas is listed as a ritual in the *Encyclopedia of Religious Rites, Rituals and Festivals* (Routledge). If your immediate reaction to the words "African ritual" is fear and judgment, deprogram the propaganda you were fed that depicts anything African as negative. This propaganda has its roots in the slave indoctrination process. Have faith that you can heal this damage, and you'll find that as you build respect for your cultural legacy, you'll feel better about yourself and find greater peace. Those seeking to become more tolerant can find interesting and sobering food for thought in another Routledge publication, the *Encyclopedia of Religion and War* (www.routledge-ny.com).

Chapter Nine
KWANZAA RESOURCES

IN this chapter you'll find out where you can attend a public Kwanzaa observance in your area, where to shop for items for your Kwanzaa table, and where to get further information on the holiday, in print or on the Internet. Included are titles of Kwanzaa CDs and extensive suggestions for other music to either play at your karamu or give as Kwanzaa gifts. If you prefer to give books or films on DVD, there are many of those listed as well, for both adults and children. A lot of information and a broad range of suggestions are provided here in the interest of helping to simplify your preparation for Kwanzaa. Use what you like and apply your enthusiasm, and a great Kwanzaa celebration is in your future.

Kwanzaa Celebrations Nationwide and International

Listed here are Kwanzaa celebrations hosted by organizations, arts institutions, cultural centers, religious and spiritual groups, universities, and businesses. Most are single-day observations, but some run through the entire seven days. Keep in mind that Kwanzaa celebrations come in all shapes and sizes; some are ideal for those who prefer casual festivities and others are best if you seek a more focused ceremony where most people are in traditional African attire. Both types of observances can be meaningful and fun, and both will likely include entertainment.

Do a little research to increase your chances of finding the right observance for you, and avoid judging by appearances alone. There are some large public gatherings, for example, where the focus is on commerce, the ceremony is Kwanzaa-lite, and the entertainment has little to do with our traditional heritage. On the other hand, an event may have seventy-five vendor tables, but also feature a substantive ceremony, enriching performing arts, and sometimes a keynote address by Dr. Karenga. Similarly, some small, community-based celebrations will provide a memorable ceremony and others will not. Ultimately, what's most important is that there is a Kwanzaa celebration in your area that you can attend. Many of these will be organized by people new to the holiday and that's wonderful—it's how Kwanzaa grows. If you're a veteran, offer to assist in the spirit of positive cooperation; if you're a new or recent observer, you may be surprised to find that your suggestions are readily welcomed. Many Kwanzaa events are free, but not all; a publicly funded or heavily endowed institution may offer a free event, whereas a small organization might charge admission to subsidize the cost of venue rental, entertainment, or speakers.

Wherever and however you participate, be sure to plan ahead. If you'll be traveling during Kwanzaa, verify the celebration details for the area you'll be visiting before you leave home.

AFRICA

Kwanzaa Celebration in Zululand. Contact Bongani Sibeko at 011 2711 482 3156.

KwanzaaCameroon's Celebration in Douala. Contact fehem@hotmail.com.

BARBADOS

Roots and Grasses Kwanzaa. Contact Ireka Jelani at (246) 431-0588 or www.rootsandgrasses.com.

CANADA

African Canadian Heritage Association. 1095 O'Connor Drive, Toronto, Ontario M4B 3M9, www.achaonline.org.

Ijo Vudu Annual Kwanzaa. In Toronto, (416) 901-1340, ijovududance.com.

Jaku Konbit Kwanzaa Celebration. Nepean, Ontario K2J-4R5, (613) 364-7998, info@jakukonbit.com.

Kwanzaa at Centennial College—Progress Campus. Markham Road and Highway 401, Toronto, Ontario, (416) 208-3149.

Ontario Black History Society. 10 Adelaide Street East, Suite 202, Toronto, Ontario, (416) 867-9420, www.blackhistorysociety.ca.

ENGLAND

A coalition of organizations hosts daily Kwanzaa events in various cities.

African United Action Front. Call 020 7503 0300.

Alkebu-Lan Kwanzaa. Call 020 8539 2154.

JLAEP and Operation Truth 2007 Kwanzaa. Malcolm X Centre, 141 City Road, Saint Pauls, Bristol.

Nottingham—Nubian Link Kwanzaa at The ACFF Centre. Beaconsfield Street, off Radford Road, Radford, Nottingham, NG7.

Pan-African Congress Movement Kwanzaa. Multiple locations have included: Kuumba 23 Hepburn Road, Saint Pauls, Bristol; Beta First (Ventura House) 47–50 Hockley Hill, Birmingham; West Indian Centre, 74 Carmoor Road, Manchester; Legends, Oxley Street, off Waterloo Road, Wolverhampton.

Call for info: 0121 554 2747, 07956 447 576, or, 0161 257 2092.

FRANCE

Association Panafricaine pour le Célébration de Kwanzaa. Hosts a Paris conference, children's Kwanzaa, and karamu, www.kwanzaa-apck.com.

JAMAICA

Wilderness House of Arts Kwanzaa. Various activities each of the seven days. Contact Ireko at (876) 994-0578.

NEW ZEALAND

Kwanzaa—The Afrikan Shop. 119 Manners Street, Wellington, 0-4-801 7773, sunflower@actrix.co.nz.

U.S. VIRGIN ISLANDS

St. Croix

Per Ankh House of Life. Call (340) 772-2654 or visit www.perankhnu.net for location and further information.

St. John

Sigma Theta Omega Chapter of Alpha Kappa Alpha Sorority Inc. Call (340) 774-3422 or (340) 690-8992 for further information.

St. Thomas

Pan African Support Group. Ital Ase Botanica Brewers Bay Beach, (340) 775-4825 or (340) 774-1318.

The African Diaspora Youth Development Foundation. Wesley Moravian Educational Complex, Tutu, (340) 776-5222.

UNITED STATES (Mainland)

Alabama

Birmingham Civil Rights Institutes Children's Pre Kwanzaa Celebration. 520 16th Street N., (866) 328-9696, www.bcri.org/index.html.

Birmingham Museum of Art. 2000 8th Avenue N., Birmingham 35203, (205) 254-2565, www.artsbma.org.

Kwanzaa Year-Round. 1045-J Hilltop Parkway, Birmingham, www.kwanzaayear-round.org/contact.html.

Alaska

Anchorage Museum of History and Art Kwanzaa Celebration. 121 West 7th Avenue, (907) 343-4326, www.anchoragemuseum.org.

Arizona

Annual East Valley Kwanzaa Celebration and Karamu. At Mesa Community College, (480) 461-7000.

Caldcleugh Multicultural Arts Center on 1700 Orchard Street. Presented by We Are One Cultural Arts Project, (336) 373-5881.

Arkansas

Griot Society and the Office of Minority Student Services Annual Kwanzaa. (501) 450-3135.

California

African American Art & Culture Complex in San Francisco. 762 Fulton Street, Suite #300, (415) 922-2049, www.aaacc.org.

AmASSI Center. 160 South La Brea Avenue, Inglewood, (310) 419-1969, www.amassi.com.

Annual Kwanzaa Karamu at the WorldBeat Cultural Center. 2100 Park Boulevard, Balboa Park, San Diego, (619) 230-1190, www.worldbeat center.org.

Bay Area Discovery Museum Annual Kwanzaa (a children's museum). 557 McReynolds Rd., Sausalito, (415) 339-3900, www.baykidsmuseum.org.

Ile Omode Kwanzaa. 8924 Holly Street, Oakland, (510) 569-2435, www.ileomode.org.

Kwanzaa Festival at Mission College. 3000 Mission College Boulevard, Santa Clara, (408) 985-8890, www.kwanzaafestival.net.

Kwanzaa Karnival in Palm Springs. Palm Springs Black History Committee. Contact Sharon McKee, (760) 329-0602, sekani2@gmail.com.

The Kwanzaa Ujima Collective, Los Angeles. Hosts annual events. Contact them at (323) 299-6124, officialkwanzaawebsite.org.

Malonga Casquelourd Center. 1428 Alice Street, Oakland, (510) 451-6100.

Marcus Book Store. 3900 MLK Boulevard, Oakland, (510) 652-2344.

Marcus Book Store. 1712 Fillmore Street, San Francisco, (415) 346-4222.

Nairobi Kwanzaa Community. 1310 Bay Road, East Palo Alto, (650) 325-5532.

Pan African Peoples Organization. 3268 San Pablo Avenue, Oakland.

Sacramento Kwanzaa Umoja Celebration. Sankofa Hall, Florin Road Arts & Business, (916) 220-5320.

Wajumbe Cultural Institution. 762 Fulton Street, San Francisco, (415) 563-3519.

Colorado

Dr. Anthony Young's Annual Kwanzaa Celebration. Hillside Community Center, 925 South Institute Street, Colorado Springs, (719) 473-6566.

100 Black Men of Denver, Inc. (303) 864-0945, www.100bmdenver.org.

Moyo Nguyu Cultural Arts Center. 160 Gilpin Street, #300, Denver, (303) 377-2511, info@afrikanarts.org.

Connecticut

African American Cultural Center. First Friday in December, Student Union Ballroom, University of Connecticut, 21110 Hillside Road, Storrs, (860) 486-3433, aacc@uconn.edu.

The Artists Collective. 1200 Albany Avenue, Hartford, (860) 527-3205, www.artistscollective.org.

The Black Student Alliance at Yale University. Afro-American Cultural Center, 211 Park Street, New Haven, (203) 432-4131.

The Bushnell Center for the Performing Arts. Twenty years of Kwanzaa, 166 Capitol Avenue, Hartford, (860) 987-5900, www.bushnell.org.

The Charter Oak Cultural Center and Sankofa Kuumba. A free Kwanzaa celebration, (860) 249-1207.

Kente Cultural Center. Events before and during Kwanzaa week, 219 Bank Street, New London, (860) 444-1955, kentecultural.org/index.html.

Stamford Kwanzaa Association. kwanzaa.wordpress.com/city-wide-locations.

Yale Kwanzaa Ball. Yale Medical School's Grand Ballroom, 367 Cedar Tree, New Haven.

Delaware

Mother African Union Church Annual Kwanzaa. 812 North Franklin Street, Wilmington, (302) 658-3838.

Florida

The Annual Spirit of Kwanzaa Celebration. Joseph Caleb Auditorium, Miami, (305) 693-6644.

Kwanzaa Kuumba Celebration. 2750 Northwest 19th Street, Fort Lauderdale, (954) 739-8498.

Pyramid Books in Boynton Beach. A source for celebration info, 544 East Gateway Boulevard, #2, Boynton Beach, (561) 731-4422, www.pyramidbooks.net.

University of Florida's Institute of Black Culture. 1510 West University Avenue, (352) 392-1261.

Georgia

Africa's Children's Fund Kwanzaa Celebration. (770) 465-6610, Stone Mountain.

APEX Museum. 135 Auburn Avenue N.E., Atlanta, (404) 523-2739, www.apexmuseum.org.

Harambee Theatre. 1312 Knotts Avenue, East Point, (404) 745-9699, www.dancical.net.

Herndon Home. 587 University Place, Atlanta, (404) 581-9813.

Kwanzaa Association's Citywide Celebration. (404) 344-1688.

Savannah Kwanzaa Committee's Kwanzaa Festival. Tompkins Center, at Ogeechee Road and 39th Street.

Shrine of the Black Madonna. 946 R.D. Abernathy Boulevard, Atlanta, (404) 752-6125, www.shrinebookstore.com.

Hawaii

The Links Inc. Family Kwanzaa Celebration. Trinity Missionary Baptist Church, 3950 Paine Circle, Honolulu, (808) 422-TMBC.

Unity Church of Hawaii Kwanzaa. 3608 Diamond Head Circle, Honolulu, (808) 735-4436.

Idaho

Idaho Black History Museum. Kids Kwanzaa, 508 Julia Davis Drive, Boise, (208) 433-0017, www.ibhm.org.

Illinois

District 65 Kwanzaa Celebration. Oakton Elementary School, 436 Ridge Avenue, Evanston, (847) 859-8800.

DuSable Museum of African American History. 740 East 56th Place, Chicago, (773) 947-0600, www.dusablemuseum.org.

Eugene B. Redmond Writing Club Annual Kwanzaa Celebration. Southern Illinois University Edwardsville, East St. Louis campus.

Malcolm X College Kwanzaa. All seven days, 1900 West Van Buren Street, Chicago, (312) 850-7000, malcolmx.ccc.edu.

National Black United Front. (312) 268-7500, ext. 154.

Trinity United Church of Christ. Several days of celebration, 400 West 95th Street, (888) 962-5650, www.tucc.org/home.htm.

Ujamaa Family Kwanzaa Market. (312) 994-1801.

Indiana

Children's Museum of Indianapolis Pre Kwanzaa Celebration. 3000 North Meridian Street, (317) 334-3322, www.childrensmuseum.org.

Indiana University Black Student Union. Karenga spoke here in 2005, Neal-Marshall Black Culture Center, (812) 855-3237, aaclib@indiana.edu.

Kwanzaa Celebration. Conley Branch Library, 1824 East Centennial, Muncie, (765) 747-8216.

Iowa

African American Historical Museum & Cultural Center of Iowa. 55 12th Avenue S.E., Cedar Rapids, (319) 862-2101 www.blackiowa.org.

Kentucky

Annual Kwanzaa Celebration. Northern Kentucky University, Office of African-American Student Affairs, (859) 572-6684.

Black Student Union University of Kentucky. Kwanzaa celebration at the Presbyterian Community Center, sassyshay97@yahoo.com.

KwanzaaFest. Organized by the Archdiocese of Louisville Multicultural Ministry, The Catholic Enrichment Center, Thea Bowman Hall, (502) 776-0262.

Louisiana

Louisiana State University, African American Cultural Center. Baton Rouge, www.lsu.edu/aacc/programs.htm.

Maine

Unitarian Universalist Church Kwanzaa. 120 Park Street, Bangor, (207) 947-7009.

Greater Bangor Area NAACP. 531 Brunswick Street, Old Town 04468.

Maryland

Baltimore Museum of Art Kwanzaa. 10 Art Museum Drive, (443) 573-1700.

Office of Community Service. 209-C Montebello Complex, Baltimore, (443) 885-4438 or (443) 885-4329.

National Great Blacks in Wax Museum. 1601-03 East North Avenue, Baltimore, (410) 563-3404, greatblacksinwax.org.

University of Maryland Annual Kwanzaa Celebration. Nyumburu Cultural Center, College Park, (301) 314-7758, www.nyumburu. umd.edu.

Massachusetts

Museum of Afro American History. 46 Joy Street, Boston 02114, (617) 367-8051, www.afroammuseum.org/events.htm.

OrigiNation Annual Kwanzaa Dance Concert. Boston, (617) 541-1875, www.originationinc.org/home.htm.

Michigan

Akwaaba Center. 8045 Second Avenue, Detroit, (313) 971-2428, www.shrinebookstore.com.

Charles H. Wright Museum of African American History. 315 East Warren Street, (313) 494-5800, www.maah-detroit.org.

Minnesota

Kwanzaa Community Church. 2100 Emerson Avenue North, Minneapolis, (612) 287-8152, www.kwanzaachurch.org.

Minnesota History Center. 345 Kellogg Boulevard, St. Paul, (651) 296-6126.

Mississippi

Jackson Kwanzaa Celebrations. Various across the city, www.visit jackson.com.

Medgar Evers Community Center. All seven days, 3159 Edwards Avenue, Jackson, (601) 960-1741.

Missouri

The Kansas City Black United Front. Annual Citywide Kwanzaa, seven days of events at the Gem Theater, 1615 East 18th Street, (816) 333-7700.

Kansas City Citywide Kwanzaa Celebration. The American Jazz Museum, (816) 474-8463, ext. 221, www.americanjazzmuseum.com.

Kwanzaa at the Missouri Botanical Garden. 4344 Shaw Boulevard, St. Louis, (314) 577-9400, www.mobot.org.

Saline County Kwanzaa. North Street Methodist Church, 365 West North Street, Marshall, (660) 886-5940.

Nebraska

Malcolm X Memorial Foundation. 3226 Lake St., Omaha, (402) 216-3695, malcolmxfoundation@gosolo.com.

Nevada

Annual Kwanzaa Celebration. West Las Vegas Arts Center, Las Vegas, (702) 229-4800.

New Jersey

Annual Kwanzaa Ball and Celebration. Also a pre-Kwanzaa fest, Rutgers University, New Brunswick Campus, (732) 932-9373 and (609) 977-4041, www.acs.rutgers.edu/events.

Annual Kwanzaa Celebration. Atlantic City Free Library, 1 North Tennessee Avenue, (609) 345-2269.

Kwanzaa Celebration at Garden State Discovery Museum. Springdale Road, #100, Cherry Hill, (856) 424-1233.

New Jersey Performing Arts Center. 36 Park Place, Newark, (888) GO-NJPAC, www.njpac.org.

Pre-Kwanzaa Celebration. Rutgers University, 5th and Cooper Streets, Camden, (856) 225-6220, cccems.rutgers.edu/MasterCalendar.

Richard Stockton College. Karenga spoke here in 2005, I-Wing Gymnasium, Pomona, (609) 652-9000, www2.stockton.edu.

New Mexico

Kwanzaa celebration. Catholic Center, St. Pius X High School, 4000 St. Joseph Place NW, Albuquerque, (505) 836-3627.

New York

Afrikan Poetry Theatre. (718) 523-3312, www.afrikapoetrytheatre.com.

Albany Kwanzaa Celebration. Shenendehowa United Methodist Church, 971 Route 146, Clifton Park, (518) 371-7964.

American Museum of Natural History. (212) 769-5315, www.amnh.org/programs.

Black Men's Exchange New York. 730 Riverside Drive, Suite 9E, Harlem, www.BMXNY.org.

College of Staten Island & Black Male Initiative of the City University of New York. At the Willowbrook campus, (718) 982-2544, or Elliott.Dawes@mail.cuny.edu.

Hamilton Hill Arts Center Annual Kwanzaa Celebration. New York State Museum, Schenectady, (518) 346-1262, www.hamiltonhillartscenter.org.

Kwanzaa at Morningstar Missionary Baptist Church. 159 Quail Street, Albany, (518) 436-7566.

Kwanzaa Collective at Boys and Girls High. 1700 Fulton Street, Brooklyn, (718) 638-6700.

The Learning Tree Cultural Center. 801 Bartholdi Street, the Bronx, (718) 947-0753, www.learningtreeprep.org.

NAKO (National Association of Kawaida Organizations). Karenga speaks annually, Boys and Girls High, 1700 Fulton Street, Brooklyn, (718) 857-0587.

OPEI Annual Kwanzaa Celebration (African Burial Ground). 290 Broadway, 30th floor, Manhattan, www.africanburialground.gov/ABG_Events.htm.

Riverbank State Park. 679 Riverside Drive, Harlem, (212) 694-3600, nysparks.state.ny.us/events.

Rochester Kwanzaa Coalition. Hosts several days, Baobab Cultural Center, 728 University Avenue, (585) 234-5926.

Rochester Kwanzaa Coalition. Montgomery Neighbhorhood Center, 10 Cady Street, (585) 436-3090 or (585) 234-5926.

Studio Museum in Harlem. 144 West 125th Street, (212) 864-4500, www.studiomuseum.org.

North Carolina

Afro-American Cultural Center. 401 North Myers Street, Charlotte, (704) 374-1565, www.aacc-charlotte.org/calendar.htm.

City of Cary Kwanzaa Celebration. Herbert C. Young Community Center, 404 North Academy Street, www.townofcary.org/depts/prdept/events/kwanzaa.htm.

Herbert C. Young Community Center. 404 North Academy Street, Cary, (919) 380-7020.

KwanzaaFest Celebration. Seven days, Hayti Heritage Center, www.hayti.org, (919) 683-1709.

KwanzaaFest Show. Hosted by African American Dance Ensemble, Durham Armory, 220 Foster Street, (919) 560-2729, www.africanamerican danceensemble.org.

The Ujima Group, Inc. (919) 460-4963.

Ohio

Afrikan-American Drum and Dance Ensemble. Hosts annual pre-Kwanzaa event. West End YMCA, 821 Ezzard Charles Drive, (513) 281-7909.

The Akron Council of Elders and the African American Cultural Association. Locations have included Stewart Afrocentric School, 1199 Vernon Odom Boulevard, (330) 873-3396. Also the Upper Room Action Ministries in West Akron.

Karamu House Annual Kwanzaa. 2355 East 89th Street, Cleveland, (216) 795-7070, www.karamu.com/home.htm.

Safiri Rites of Passage Program Annual Kwanzaa Ceremony. Cleveland, contact Sekhmet Nefertari Lee-Ivey at JLeeIvey@mail.ignatius.edu.

Oklahoma

Ralph Ellison Library. 2000 N.E. 23rd Street, Oklahoma City, (405) 424-1437.

Oregon

Black Student Union at Lewis and Clark College (check for nonstudent attendance). Templeton Student Center, Stamm Building, Portland, guwagbae@lclark.edu.

The Bridge Builders Annual Kwanzaa Gala and Rites of Passage Ceremony. At the Portland Center for the Performing Arts, (503) 248.4335.

Willamette University Black Students Union Kwanzaa in Salem. Contact Multicultural Affairs, (503) 370-6265, www.willamette.edu/dept/oma/events.

Pennsylvania

African American Museum Pre Kwanzaa Celebration. 701 Arch Street, Philadelphia, (215) 574-0380, www.aampmuseum.org/events.

The City of Chester Annual Kwanzaa Celebration. (610) 872-5328.

HACC Campus Annual Kwanzaa Festival. Harrisburg, (717) 780-2632, pjthomps@hacc.edu.

The Kwanzaa Cooperative. Hosts several days, 1542 Fontaine Street, Philadelphia 19121, (215) 769-7324.

Penn State Black Graduate Student Association Annual Kwanzaa. (814) 865-9795, www.clubs.psu.edu/up/bgsa.

Yeadon Annual Kwanzaa. More than a decade of celebrations at Yeadon Borough Hall, Church Lane and Bailey Road.

Rhode Island

A Kwanzaa Song. Annual evening-length production in Pawtucket, The Mixed Magic Theatre Exult Choir, Tolman High School Auditorium, Bristol Community College, 150 Exchange Street, (401) 722-1881.

South Carolina

Avery Research Center at the College of Charleston. 125 Bull Street, Charleston, (843) 953-7609, www.cofc.edu/avery/index.htm.

The Kemet School of Myrtle Beach. For information, call (843) 669-3013.

Kwanzaa Celebration March and Feast. Mall Park to St. Julian Community Center, Charleston, www.charlestoncity.info.

Trident Technical College. 7000 Rivers Avenue, North Charleston, (877) 349-7184, www.tridenttech.edu/94.htm.

Winthrop University Kwanzaa Celebration. Karenga spoke here in 2005, Tillman Auditorium, Rock Hill, (803) 323-2211, ext. 4524.

Tennessee

African American Cultural Alliance Kwanzaa. Gordon Memorial Church, 2334 Herman Street, Nashville, (615) 251-0007, www.africanamericanculturalalliance.com/calendar.htm.

SACCA (Society for African-American Cultural Awareness) Annual Kwanzaa. Jackson, (731) 616-0814, www.saaca.com.

Texas

The Children's Museum of Houston. 1500 Binz Street, Houston, (713) 522-1138, ext 208, www.cmhouston.org.

The Greater Houston Kwanzaa Planning Committee. Contact S.H.A.P.E. Center, (713) 521-0629, www.shape.org.

Kwanzaa Fest. Annual Kwanzaa Festival at Fair Park, Dallas, www.fairpark.org.

McCall Neighborhood Center Kwanzaa. 3231 Wyoming Avenue, El Paso, (915) 566-2407.

Nia Cultural Center's Kwanzaa. Galveston, (409) 765-7086, niacultural@sbcglobal.net.

SHAPE Community Center Kwanzaa Celebration. Houston, (713) 521-7629, www.shape.org/Kwanzaa.asp.

Shrine of the Black Madonna. 5309 M. L. King Boulevard, Houston, (713) 645-1071, www.shrinebookstore.com.

Utah

Utah Museum of Fine Arts Annual Kwanzaa. At the Middle East Center, Orson Spencer Hall, 260 South Central Campus Drive, Room 153, University of Utah, Salt Lake City, (801) 581-5003.

Vermont

First Unitarian Universalist Society of Burlington Annual Kwanzaa Celebration. 152 Pearl Street, Burlington, (802) 862-5630, www.uusociety.org.

Virginia

Capital City Kwanzaa Festival. Hosted by Elegba Folklore Society, Richmond, (804) 644-3900, www.elegbafolkloresociety.org/efs_festivals.html.

Kwanzaa Celebration. Norfolk Public Library, www.hamptonroads.com.

Norfolk/Hampton Annual Kwanzaa Celebration. www.imanifoundation.com or www.hamptonroads.com.

Washington

African American Museum. Tacoma, www.aamuseumtacoma.org.

Seattle Center Kwanzaa Celebration. www.seattlecenter.com.

Washington D.C.

African American Holiday Association. Kwanzaa celebration resource, aaha-info.org.

Smithsonian Museum's Kwanzaa Celebrations. At various locations, including: National Museum of African American Art, National Museum of Natural History, Anacostia Museum, and Center for African American History and Culture, www.si.edu/events.

24-hour Kwanzaa Line. Continuous updates of numerous celebrations districtwide at (202) 310-1430.

West Virginia

The West Virginia University Center for Black Culture and Research. An annual Kwanzaa celebration, (304) 293-7029.

Wisconsin

Milwaukee Public Museum. 800 West Wells Street, Milwaukee, (414) 278 2728, www.mpm.edu.

Kujichagulia Lutheran Center Kwanzaa at the Capitol Library. 3969 North 74th Street, (414) 286-3006.

The Wisconsin Black Historical Society. 2620 West Center Street, (414) 372-7677, www.wbhsm.org/welcome.htm.

Visit www.tike.com, www.blackwebportal.com/tidbits/Kwanzaa.cfm, and www.soulofamerica.com/events/kwanzaa.html for updated Kwanzaa event listings.

Kwanzaa Information Online

www.kwanzaabook.com. A site for this book and related information.

melanet.com/kwanzaa. Kwanzaa Information Center.

www.officialkwanzaawebsite.org. Dr. Maulana Karenga's site.

www.swagga.com/kwanzaa.htm. Information, instructions, photos, and resources.

www.tike.com. The International Kwanzaa Exchange.

Kwanzaa-Themed Music

B'lieve I'll Run On (See What the End's Gonna Be), **by Sweet Honey in the Rock**. Redwood Records, 1978. Has the beautiful "Seven Principles." Rare, order online.

The Drummer's Path, **by Sule Greg Wilson.** www.drumpath.net. Drummers' tutorial and good background music for a Kwanzaa karamu.

The Essence of Kwanzaa, **by Bill Summers.** Monkey Hill, 1997. Nguzo Saba songs in jazz, Afro beat, funk, and club music.

In My Soul, **by Four the Moment.** Jam Productions Ltd. Has a lovely Nguzo Saba a cappella song. Rare, search online.

Introducing Maia, **by Maia.** The Orchard, 2001. Features "Kujichagulia" and "Happy Kwanzaa."

Invocations for Kwanzaa **by Jacqueline Godden Silver Bush Music (a 2-CD set).**

The Kwanzaa Album, **by Women of the Calabash.** Bermuda Reefs, 1998. Great energy and diversity of musical style.

Kwanzaa Ceremonial Music, **by** Ama & Wafafanisha, Afi. December 1999.

Kwanzaa Music: A Celebration of Black Cultures in Song, **compiled by Eric Copage.,** Rounder Records. 1994. Fabulous! My favorite! Order locally or through Amazon.com.

Kwanzaa Party, **compiled by Eric Copage.** Rounder Records, 1996. Order through your local store or Amazon.com.

Libation for Our Ancestors: A Family and Communal Activity at Kwanzaa. Tarik Karenga, a how-to with some music. www.tarikkarenga.com/products.html.

More Than a Month, **by Zahmu.** www.morethanmonth.com, contains "It's Kwanzaa Time!" and Black history songs.

Seven Principles, **by Steve Cobb and Chavunduka.** Cobbala, 2004, www.cobbala.com. Polished, diverse genres, great vocals.

Sounds of Kwanzaa, **various artists.** Glenauldbin Music, 2001. Reggae and jazz, some strong cuts, may have to search for it.

Wicked Funk, **by Kwanzaa Posse, also *Musika*.** Tribal house for a karamu. Search discogs.gemm.com and www.plastikfantastik.nl.

Words of Power from Planet Afrika, **by Imhotep Gary Byrd & the GBE.** Worldwide GBE. Electric Publishing, Inc., 1995. Contains "Kwanzaa—Nguzo Saba."

Kwanzaa Music for Children

Everybody Loves Kwanzaa, **by Ankh Ra Amenhetep.** Humility Music, Inc., humilitymusic.com. *Everybody* is celebratory and engages children.

Kwanzaa Folktales (audiobook), by Jonelle Allen, Angela Bassett, John Whitman.

Kwanzaa for Young People (and Everyone Else!), various artists. Orchard, 1999, a song for each principle.

Kwanzaa Sing-Along, various artists. Peter Pan (ISP), August 2006, www.cduniverse.com. Search under label name.

A Magical Musical Celebration of Kwanzaa (a play on tape with rehearsal songbooks), by Aduke Aremu and Ben Steifel, www.kamkyi books.com/sourceintl/kwanzaa.html.

The Nguzo Saba: The Seven Principles of Kwanzaa, **by Kwanzaa Media.** Also Kwanzaa Kwest video and interactive CD, www.kwanzaa media.com.

For a wide selection of African music, see music.calabashmusic.com/ world/africa.

Other Music for Gift-Giving, a Karamu, or a Self-Made Mix

The titles listed here are all over the map (literally and figuratively); some are standards, or should have been standards, and others are from new artists. It's just a sampling, as there is so much more great music than space to mention. Music from Africa is included and is always a wonderful companion to a Kwanzaa gathering. These selections are not, for the most part, grouped in categories such as "jazz," and "reggae," because it's hoped that readers will not go automatically to the familiar, while overlooking other suggestions.

Music for Children

***African American Folk Songs & Rhythms, Jambo & Other Call and Response Songs and Chants, and Call-And-Response: Rhythmic Group Singing,* all by Ella Jenkins.** World-recognized rhythm specialist Ella Jenkins is called "Queen of Children's Music."

African Lullaby, various artists. Beautiful music to get the little ones to settle down—on Ellipsis Arts.

African Playground, Caribbean Playground,* and *Reggae Playground. Wonderful music from top artists on these three from the Putumayo Kids Series.

Blues for Kids Sake, various artists. Chicago singers and musicians donated proceeds, www.bbbswillgrundy.org/bluesCD.htm.

Celebration of Soul. James Brown, Jackson 5, etc., make little feet move, store.musicforlittlepeople.com.

***Choo Choo Boogaloo,* by Buckwheat Zydeco.** Accordions in a rollicking Mardi Gras party, store.musicforlittlepeople.com.

DJ's Choice: Reggae for Kids. Lively favorites make for lots of fun! www.cduniverse.com.

The Gift of the Tortoise, **by Ladysmith Black Mambazo.** Songs, stories, and those voices!

I Got Shoes and All for Freedom, **by Sweet Honey in the Rock.** Fun, funny, socially aware, and infectious songs about childhood—Kids love 'em!

Jazz for Kids: Sing, Clap, Wiggle and Shake. Ella, Louis, Carmen, Lionel, and others sing things like "Old MacDonald."

Kids Get the Blues Too/Blues for Beginners, **by Brother Yusef.** Familiar songs such as "This Old Man" and "Hush Little Baby" get the blues treatment.

More Reggae for Kids, various artists. Bunny Wailer, Gregory Issacs, and more.

The Rough Guide to African Music for Children. Great artists and a variety of instruments from across the continent.

Songhai Djeli: Folktales. Absorbing African tales, captivating melodies, lots of rhythm, www.songhaidjeli.com.

Songs for the Young at Heart, **by Taj Mahal.** Blues and world music, store.musicforlittlepeople.com.

Sweet Honey in the Rock: Singing for Freedom **(DVD).** The amazing ladies live at a children's concert! Little ones can sing along.

Treblemakers Jazz It Up! **by the Treblemakers Children's Choir.** Jazzed-up nursery rhymes and folk songs, cdbaby.com/cd/treblemakers3.

Music for Adults and Families

Adventures in Afropea 3: Telling Stories to the Sea. Warner Bros./WEA, 1995. Gorgeous Afro-Portuguese music.

Africa (Live), **by Miriam Makeba, also Sangoma.** Novus, 1991, and Warner Bros/WEA, 1998. Some of her most beautiful and powerful.

Amandla! A Revolution in Four-Part Harmony **(the film soundtrack).** Authentic South African music with some amazing vocals, www.amandla.com.

The Anthology 1961–1977, **by Curtis Mayfield, also** *New World Order.* MCA, 1992, and Warner Bros, 1996. Great compilation and the master's final work.

Aretha Franklin: 30 Greatest Hits, **also** *Live at the Fillmore West.* Atlantic/WEA, 1985, and Rhino/Wea, 2006. It's Aretha—'nuff said! Long live the queen!

Ballads, **by Elvin Jones with Coltrane, Garrison, Tyner, and Workman.** Grp Records, 1995, remastered. Sublime!

Bee Hold Her **and** *Soul Belly Dance Experience,* **by Sahuspit.** Indie release, 2005, 2007, touchup27@aol.com. Spiritual uplift, airy vocals and rhythm.

Belafonte and Miriam Makeba, **by Harry Belafonte and Miriam Makeba.** BMG Intl., 2003. Lovely South African folk songs.

The Best of Dianne Reeves, **also** *Bridges.* Blue Note, 2002 and 1999. *Best* has deeply satisfying work, *Bridges* goes new places.

The Best of Steel Pulse (20th Century), **also,** *Earth Crisis, Vex, and African Holocaust.* Hip-O, Wise Man Doctrine, MCA, and others. A long and strong career in reggae.

Black Is, **by Fertile Ground, also** *Seasons Change* **and** *Spiritual War.* Pony Canyon, 2004, Blackout Studios, 2002, and the Orchard, 2000. Danceable uplift.

Black Power: Music of a Revolution, **various artists.** Shout Factory, 2004. Popular and obscure greats and small samples of speeches.

Bird of Paradise, **by Djavan.** Sony (on CD, 1990). Wonderful young Brazilian artist.

Borders of Disorderly Time, **by Jayne Cortez and the Firespitters.** Jayne Cortez/Bola Press, 2003, www.jaynecortez.com. Veteran poet with jazz backup.

Brother, Brother, Brother, **by The Isley Brothers, also** *Givin' It Back and It's Your Thing.* Sony, 1972, 1971, and 1999. All their greatests! *Givin'* has the rare "Ohio/Machine Gun."

Chapter Two, **by Roberta Flack, also** *Roberta.* Atlantic/WEA, 1970, and 1994. Chapter is phenomenal. Roberta has jazz and standards.

The Colored Section, **by Donnie.** Motown, 2002. Great talent and "Big Black Buck" is a Kujichagulia song!

Destination Motherland, **by Roy Ayers,** *Music of Many Colors,* **and** *Mahogany Vibe.* Universal International, 2003 (a 2-disc compilation), and M.I.L. Multimedia, 1986.

Drums of Passion, **by Olatunji,** *also Healing Session.* Narada, 2003. *Drums* is the original masterpiece, and *Healing* is just that.

Eastern Sounds, **by Yusef Lateef.** Prestige, 2006 (remastered). Beautiful, soul-awakening sound.

Equal Rights, **by Peter Tosh.** Sony, 1999. A classic from one of the original Wailers.

Essential Sly and the Family Stone. Sony, 2003. Big fun, small gems, irresistible music from one of the greatest bands ever!

Full Moon of Sonia, **by Sonia Sanchez.** VIA International Artists, Inc., www.viaartists.com. The poet icon now has a band!

Get on the Bus, **various artists, from and inspired by the movie.** Interscope, 1996. Stevie, Curtis, Kirk Franklin, Guru, Marc Dorsey's "Welcome" etc.

Higher Consciousness, **by Ankh Ra Amenhetep.** Humility Music, Inc., humilitymusic.com. High-energy message music for entertaining or every day.

Hope (Live), **by Hugh Masakela, also** *Black to the Future.* Triloka Records, 1993, and Shanachie, 1999. South African jazz with a funk groove.

Inside Betty Carter, **also** *I'm Yours, You're Mine* **and many others.** Blue Note, Polygram, and others. Breathtakingly beautiful and inventive jazz vocals.

JB40: 40th Anniversary Collection, **by James Brown.** Polygram, 1996. Essential for an R&B collection. Better reviewed than the 50th.

John Coltrane and Johnny Hartman. GRP Records, 1995, remastered. Too beautiful for words!

Journey Through the Secret Life of Plants, **by Stevie Wonder, and his other wonders.** Motown on CD, 1992 (on vinyl 1979). An overlooked concept masterpiece and great gift.

Karma **by Pharoah Sanders, features "The Creator Has a Master Plan."** GRP Records, 1995. Beautiful, mind-blowing feat. Give to open minds.

Kulanjan, **by Taj Mahal and Toumani Diabate.** Hannibal, 1999. Blues meets the kora playing of Africa. Beautiful with a sense of humor.

The Legend—The Best of the Last Poets. M.I.L. Multimedia, 1996. Thirty-eight tracks make this a formidable collection.

A Long Way from Normal, **by Awadagin Pratt, also** *Live from South Africa.* Angel Records, 1994, and EMI Classics, 1997. Relatively unsung classical concert pianist.

A Love Supreme, **by John Coltrane, also** *My Favorite Things* **and many others.** Impulse (orig. 1964) and Atlantic/WEA (orig. 1960). Just two by a jazz genius.

Medase and *Rise Vision Comin,* **by Haki Madhubuti.** Visionary and inspiring poetry and music, www.thirdworldpressinc.com.

Million Man Music, **by Songhai Djeli.** Jazz and percussion with positive, heritage-focused lyrics, www.songhaidjeli.com.

Mind Adventures, **by Des'Ree, also** *I Ain't Movin'* **(featuring "You Gotta Be").** Sony, 1992. Two lovely CDs to own or give, but skip *Supernatural.*

The Miseducation of Lauryn Hill, **by Lauryn Hill.** Sony, 1998. A classic from a gifted artist, succeeds on all levels.

Mmalo-We, **by Bayete and Jabu Khanyile.** Mango, 1995. Beautiful and danceable music and vocals from South Africa.

New Moon Daughter, **by Cassandra Wilson, also** *Travelin' Miles* **and**

Blue Skies. Blue Note, 1996, Blue Note, 1999, and Polygram, 1988. Smart, smoky, jazzy, bluesy magic.

***Plantation Lullabies,* by Meshell N'degeOcello and others.** Maverick, 1993. One captivating, controversial, bass-playing sista with that voice . . .

The Once and Future,* by The Jazzyfatnastees, also *The Tortoise and the Hare. MCA, 1999, and Coolhunter, 2002. Refreshing, positive, overlooked young sisters.

***Osunlade Presents Yoruba Records: 5 Years Later,* by Osunlade.** Yoruba, 2006. House mix for dance parties.

Patti LaBelle—Greatest Hits,* also *Live! One Night Only. MCA, 1996 and 1998. A well-considered collection and a wonderful concert CD.

Primal Roots,* by Sergio Mendes, also *Timeless. Universal/A&M. They finally rereleased this Brazilian beauty! Also Concord, 2006.

***Q: The Musical Biography of Quincy Jones,* a 4-CD boxed set.** Rhino/Wea, 2001. Expensive, but wow! Worth it for the creative example alone.

Ray Charles and Betty Carter: Dedicated to You. Rhino/WEA, 1998. Duets and also Ray singing solo. Has "Baby, It's Cold Outside."

***Red Hot and Riot,* various artists.** MCA, 2002. Fabulous Fela tribute with proceeds benefiting AIDS work in Africa.

***Red Hot on Impulse,* various artists.** GRP Record, 1994. Truly, unique and beautiful. The Coltranes, Mingus, Shepp, etc.

Reverence,* by Richard Bona, also *Tiki. Sony, Decca. Cameroon bassist and vocalist offers authentic Afro-Cuban, jazz, etc.

Rooms in My Fatha's House,* by Vinx, also *This Mood I'm In. Capitol, 1999. Gifted percussionist and songwriter with a beautiful voice.

Roy Ayers Evolution: The Polydor Anthology. Polydor, 1995. Showcases the great vibraphonist's jazz, funk, and R&B chops.

Sam Cooke Portrait of a Legend 1951–1964,* also *The Rhythm and the Blues. ABKCO, 2003, and RCA, 1995. Portrait has the hits and more. *Rhythm* has nice surprises.

***Sarah Vaughn with Clifford Brown*, also *Golden Hits*.** Polygram, 2000 (original, 1954) and 1990 (original, 1958). Melt with pleasure!

***Say It Loud! A Celebration of Black Music in America*, various artists.** Rhino/WEA, 2001. Louis, Miles, Ray, Otis, Aretha, Curtis, you name it.

***Serious Business*, by Third World, also *Third World Live* and *Reggae Ambassadors*.** Beatsville, 2001, Polygram, 1989, and Mercury, 1993. Conscious reggae band, classic hits.

***7* and *A Ma Zone* and *Ancestry in Progress*, by Zap Mama.** Luaka Bop, 2004. Fabulous talents singing in French and English.

***Sonny, Please*, by Sonny Rollins, also *The Bridge*, *Saxophone Colossus*, and others.** The first release on his own label, www.sonnyplease.com, also OJC label and others.

***Spirits Known and Unknown*, by Leon Thomas.** BMG International, 2004. Deep-throated, globally inspired jazz singer and chanter.

***Still on the Journey*, by Sweet Honey in the Rock, *Sacred Ground*, *Selections*, and more.** Earthbeat! Order at its sister site: store.musicfor littlepeople.com/sw.html.

***Survival*, by Bob Marley, also *Rastaman Vibration*, *One Love*.** Island, 2001, and UMVD, 2001.

***Tenderness*, by Al Jarreau, also *Accentuate the Positive* and others.** Warner Bros./Wea, Verve. The velvety, elastic, jazz vocalist. Mellow and passionate.

***Testimony, Vol. 1, Life & Relationship*, India.Arie, also *Acoustic Soul*, *Voyage to India*.** UMVD, 2006, and Motown. Lovely, memorable, and positive music, great gift for teens.

***There's a Music in the Air*, by Letta Mbulu.** Universal/Polygram, 2001 (remastered). One of the South African queens of song.

***These Songs for You (Live)*, by Donny Hathaway, also *A Donny Hathaway Collection*.** Atlantic/WEA, 1990, and 2004. *Songs* has an interview; *Collection* has other best titles.

Traveling the Spaceways, **by Ahmed Abdullah's Dispersions of the Spirit of RA.** Planet Arts Recordings, 2004. Great jazz, some with poetry, in tribute to Sun Ra.

Truth Is on Its Way, **by Nikki Giovanni.** Collectables. Nikki's incisive social commentary over gospel music made a classic.

20th Century Piano Genius, **by Art Tatum, also** *The Best of Art Tatum.* Polygram, 1996, and Pablo, 1987. Wonderful for your jazz collection.

*Upside Down, Shakara, Expensive S**T,* **and everything else by Fela Anikulapo Kuti.** MCA, 2000. The Afro Beat pioneer genius! *Expensive* has "Water No Get Enemy." Bliss!

Very Best of Caiphus Semenya. Sony Globetrotter—Sterns, 1999. This South African icon worked with Quincy and Nina.

Very Best of Nina Simone, The Best of Nina Simone, **and many others.** Bmg, May 2006, and Polygram, 1990 (original, 1964). Your life just got better!

A Turtle's Dream, **by Abbey Lincoln, also** *Devil's Got Your Tongue* **and others.** Polygram, 1995 and 1993. Wise and wonderful music from a truly unique talent.

What's Goin On, **by Marvin Gaye, also** *The Very Best of Marvin Gaye.* Motown, 2003 and 2001 (remastered). The forever classic and a wide-ranging review.

World Music, **by Taj Mahal.** Sony, 1993. A formidable talent masters the music of the African Diaspora.

Volunteered Slavery, **by Rahsaan Roland Kirk, also** *Brotherman in the Fatherland.* Collectables, 2002, and HYENA Records, 2006. Genius jazz with personality and humor.

Year of the Endless Moment, **by The Moving Form.** Engine Studios, 2004, engine-studios.com. Innovative and accomplished jazz and poetry.

Yellow Moon, **by The Neville Brothers, also** *Walking in the Shadow of Life.* A&M Records, 1990, and Back Porch, 2004. Some of the best by some of the best.

Again, there are musical greats and talented newcomers not listed above, so consider also work by the following artists, taking time to first listen online to snippets of those who are new to you, as these represent a wide range of musical styles and tastes:

Ali Farka Toure, Salif Keita, Charlie Parker, Charles Mingus, Youssou N'dour, Baba Maal, The Mahotella Queens, Manu Dibango, Femi Kuti, Public Enemy, Michael Rose, Black Uhuru, Burning Spear, Sister Carol, Thomas Mapfumo, Issac Hayes, Thelonious Monk, Sekou Sundiata, The Roots, Jill Scott, Isley Brothers, Leela James, Young Disciples, Heritage O.P., Floetry, Van Hunt, Amp Fiddler, Al Green, Otis Redding, Billie Holiday, Sade, Speech, Nat King Cole, Arrested Development, Kindred, The Family Stand, Sekou Sundiata, Carl Hancock Rux, Camille Yarbrough, Saul Williams, Nana Soul, Mary Mary, Caron Wheeler, The Fugees, Vieux Diop, Quartette Indigo, Lizz Wright, Anita Baker, and Wyclef Jean.

The following CDs have tracks that may interest teens in hip hop's original mission to have fun while provoking thought, as compared with the materialistic and misogynistic variety that is universally promoted today. Included here are both classics and new releases. Some of these CDs, however, contain tracks with "clean" lyrics as well as others which contain explicit material and/or the "N word." Consider listening to and then purchasing individual tracks of your choice on the Internet and making your own CD as a gift to a young person.

Be, by Common. Geffen Records, 2005.

Black on Both Sides, by Mos Def. Priority Records, 1999.

Black Star, by Mos Def and Talib Kweli. Rawkus (Uni), 1998.

Blazing Arrow, by Blackalicious. MCA, 2002.

Eric B. and Rakim: Gold. Hip-O Records, 2005.

Game Theory, by The Roots. Def Jam, 2006.

Here Comes the Sun, by Faro Z. Live Era, 2006, www.myspace.com/thesunman.

Lyrics of Sunshine and Shadow, by Red Dragon. www.myspace.com/reddragonbklyn.

Mind Over Matter, by Zion I. Ground Control, 2000.

New Horizon, by Supanova. D1 Music, 2005.

Reflection Eternal/Train of Thought, by Talib Kweli and Hi-Tek. Rawkus, 2002.

She's a Queen: A Collection of Hits, by Queen Latifah. Motown, 2002.

St. Elsewhere, by Gnarls Barkley. Downtown, 2006.

You've browsed suggestions for guests and gifts, now here's something for you—catch up with a musical legend at www.phatta datta.com.

Books: The Perennial Kwanzaa Gift

Books are one of the most favored of the traditional Kwanzaa gifts. This section offers a number of suggestions that will make great gifts. Included are books on Kwanzaa and fiction, nonfiction, essay, and poetry titles. The listing is extensive because it's meant to be used as a tool for readers seeking books for themselves. The nonfiction books explore a wide range of issues and provide information and perspectives for those committing to a year-round observance of the Seven Principles. The fiction and poetry books can help to enrich our understanding of the Black experience. Other books are included just because they're great fun. By no means should readers think this author has read all these books: many are recommended from personal experience and many more are on my to-do list, so let's read together.

Children's books are listed first, and included is a recommended reading list by a woman mentioned earlier in this book who is a super teacher and staff- and curriculum-developer. There are also historical and cultural games included at the close of the children's listing.

Kwanzaa Books for Children

Between Father and Son, by Eric Copage (formerly *A Kwanzaa Fable).*
Celebrating Kwanzaa, by Diane Hoyt-Goldsmith, et al.
The Children's Book of Kwanzaa, by Dolores Johnson.
Classic Kwanzaa Poems: New and Collected, by Johnnie Renee Nelson.
The Gifts of Kwanzaa, by Synthia Saint James.
Habari Gani: What's the News? by Sundaira Morninghouse.
Imani's Gift at Kwanzaa, by Denise Burden-Patmon.
It's Kwanzaa Time! by Linda and Clay Goss.
K is for Kwanzaa: A Kwanzaa Alphabet Book, by Juwanda G. Ford.
Kwanzaa: A Family Affair, by Mildred Pitts Walker.
Kwanzaa! Africa Lives in a New World Festival, by Sule Greg C. Wilson.
Kwanzaa Celebration: Pop-Up Book, by Nancy Williams.
Kwanzaa Fun: Great Things to Make and Do, by Linda Robertson.
Kwanzaa Karamu: Cooking and Crafts for a Kwanzaa Feast, by April A. Brady.
The Kwanzaa Sticker Activity Book, by Cheryl Willis Hudson and Sylvia Walker.
Let's Celebrate Kwanzaa (Activity Book), by Helen Davis.
Mommy Is It Kwanzaa Yet? by Barbara Ann Johnson-Stokes.
My First Kwanzaa Book, by Deborah M. Newton Chocolate et al.
Seven Candles for Kwanzaa, by Andrea Davis Pinkney.
Seven Spools of Thread, by Angela Shelf Medearis.
The Story of Kwanzaa, by Safisha L. Madhubuti.
The Story of Kwanzaa, by Donna L. Washington.
Together for Kwanzaa, by Juwanda G. Ford and Shelly Hehenberger.

Other Children's Books for Gift-Giving

The Afro Bets, Kid Caramel, and others, Just Us Books, www.justusbooks.com.
Amazing Grace, by Mary Hoffman.
The Big Box, and other books by Toni Morrison.
Black Americans of Achievement Series, by Chelsea House Publications.
Danitra Brown Leaves Town, Nikki Grimes and Floyd Cooper.
Dear Corinne, Tell Somebody! Love Annie: A Book About Secrets, by Mari Evans.
Earth Mother, by Ellen Jackson, illustrated by Leo and Dianne Dillon.
Ellington Was Not a Street, by Ntozake Shange.
Hewitt Anderson's Great Big Life, by Jerdine Nolen.
Hush, by Jacqueline Woodson.
Huggy Bean and the Origin of the Magic Kente Cloth, by Linda Cousins.
If a Bus Could Talk: The Story of Rosa Parks, by Faith Ringgold.
I Have a Dream, various by Scholastic.
Jambo Means Hello, and other books by Tom and Muriel Feelings.
Jazzy Miz Mozetta, by Brenda C. Roberts.
The Journey of Henry Box Brown, by Karyn Parsons (with CD narrated by Alfre Woodard).
Kheru Nefer: Beautiful Night, Spirit Publishing LLC, www.spiritEF.com.
Kofi and His Magic, by Maya Angelou.
Let It Shine: Stories of Black Women Freedom Fighters, by Andrea Davie Pinkney.
Let the Circle Be Unbroken, by Mildred D. Taylor.
Moses: When Harriet Tubman Led Her People to Freedom, by Carol Boston Weatherford.
My Painted House, My Friendly Chicken and Me, by Maya Angelou.
Mufaro's Beautiful Daughters, and other books by John Steptoe.
Portraits of African-American Heroes, by Ansel Pitcairn.
The People Could Fly, and other books by Virginia Hamilton.
Rosa, by Nikki Giovanni and Bryan Collier.
The Six Fools, based on a Zora Neale Hurston story, illustrated by Ann Tanksley.

*Add almost anything illustrated by Tom Feelings or Leo and Dianne Dillon.

Trapped Between the Lash and the Gun, by Arvella Whitmore.
Very Young Poets, by Gwendolyn Brooks.

If you'd like to educate your child or students about problems faced by children in parts of Africa, visit the Web site of the UN Refugee Agency to request sample copies of children's books on young refugees and child soldiers. Although the colorful illustrations are captivating, these stories are straightforward, so read along with your child (www.unhcr.org/cgi-bin/texis/vtx/help?id=408384197).

Self-Esteem and Acceptance

Annie's Gifts, by Angela Shelf Medearis.
Be Boy Buzz, by bell hooks.
Bright Eyes, Brown Skin, by Cheryl Willis Hudson.
Colors Around Me, by Vivian Church and Sherman Beck.
Girls Hold Up This World, by Jada Pinkett Smith.
Grandpa, Is Everything Black Bad? by Sandy Lynne Holman.
Happy to Be Nappy, by bell hooks.
I Like Myself, by Karen Beaumont.
I Look at Me, by Mari Evans.
I'm African and Proud, by Jwajiku Korantemaa, www.africanandproud.com.
Nappy Hair, by Carolivia Herron.
Nina Bonita, by Anna Maria Machado.
No Mirrors in My Nana's House (with musical CD), by Ysaye M. Barnwell, illustrated by Synthia Saint James.
The Skin I'm In, by Sharon G. Flake.
The Skin We're In, by Janie Victoria Ward.
Shades of Black, by Sandra L. Pinkney.
When I Look in My Mirror, by Sopoeia Greywolf.
Wild, Wild Hair, by Nikki Grimes.

Teens

African Beginnings and *Bound for America: The Forced Migration of Africans to the New World,* by James Haskins and Kathleen Benson.
Freedom's Children: Young Civil Rights Activists Tell Their Own Stories, by Ellen Levine.
Hoops, by Walter Dean Myers.
I Know Why the Caged Bird Sings, by Maya Angelou.
Letters to a Young Artist, by Anna Deveare Smith.
Letters to a Young Brother, by Hil Harper.
The Long Journey Home: Stories from Black History, by Julius Lester.
Middle Passage, with an introduction by Dr. John Henrik Clarke.
The Pact and We Beat the Street: How a Friendship Led to Success, by Sampson Davis, George Jenkins, Rameck Hunt, Sharon M. Draper.
The Scottsboro Boys, by James Haskins.
Stay Strong: Simple Life Lessons for Teens, by Terrie Williams.
Sugar in the Raw: Voices of Young Black Girls in America, by Rebecca Carroll.
33 Things Every Girl Should Know, by Tonya Bolden.

Teen Fiction

Between Father and Son: An African American Fable, by Eric Copage.
Bronx Masquerade, by Nikki Grimes.
Copper Sun, Tears of a Tiger and other books, by Sharon M. Draper.
Daughter, by Asha Bandele.
I Hadn't Meant To Tell You This, and other books by Jacqueline Woodson.
The First Part Last, by Angela Johnson.
Kindred, by Octavia Butler.
Like Sisters on the Homefront, by Rita Williman-Garcia.
Monster, and other books by Walter Dean Myers.
Spellbound, by Janet McDonald.
Who Am I Without Him?: Short Stories About Girls and the Boys in Their Lives, by Sharon G. Flake.

Nazalima's List: Great Books of All Kinds for Children

For Younger Readers (K–3)

Allie's Basketball Dream, by Barbara E. Barber.
Boundless Grace, by Mary Hoffman.
Do Like Kyla, by Angela Johnson.
Flowers for Mommy, by Susan Anderson.
The Honest to Goodness Truth and *Flossie and the Fox,* by Pat Mckissack.
Jamaica Finds series, by Juanita Havill.
Jamal's Busy Day, by Wade Hudson.
The Jones Family Express, by Javaka Steptoe.
Little Bill series, by Bill Cosby.
Regina's Big Mistake, by Marissa Moss.
Something Beautiful, by Sharon Dennis Wyeth.
Shortcut, by Donald Crews.
Stevie, by John Steptoe.
Willimena Rules series: *How to Lose Your Class Pet* and *How to Fish for Trouble,* by Valerie Wilson Wesley.

Older Readers (Grades 3–6)

The Dear One, by Jacqueline Woodson.
Gold Cadillac, by Mildred Taylor.
Hoops and Darnell Rock Reporting, by Walter Dean Myers.
Julian Tales series, by Ann Cameron.
Kid Caramel series, and *Captain Africa,* by Dwyane Ferguson.
Neate Series and *Elizabeth's Wish,* by Debbi Chocolate.
Shimmershine Queens, by Camille Yarbrough.
Sister, by Eloise Greenfield.
Strong to the Hoop, by John Coy.
Talk About a Family, by Eloise Greenfield.
Ziggy and the Black Dinosaurs series, by Sharon M. Draper.

All Ages

African Tales, by Hugh Vernon Jackson.
A Band of Angels, by Deborah Hopkinson.

Barefoot, by Escape on the Underground Railroad.
Childtimes, by Eloise Greenfield.
Clean Your Room Harvey Moon, by Pat Cummings.
Visiting Day, by Jacqueline Woodson.
Visiting Langston, by Willie Perdomo.
Rent Party Jazz, by William Miller.

Board Games and Playing Cards

Afro-Centric XWORDZ & Puzzlez, by Kanes Publications
Black America History Blackboard, by Peter Reilly Innovative Designs
Black History Playing Card Deck, by Deloris L. Holt
Black History Trivia Game
Black Quest
Famous African Americans J-I-N-G-O, by Gary Grimm
I Can Do Anything
Journey to the Motherland
Knowledge Cards (playing cards): Great African Americans, Civil Rights Movement
Littleafrica.com/games, a games source
Motownopply
My First Matching Game
Ndinga!
Who Am I?

Kwanzaa-Related Books for Adults

The Complete Kwanzaa: Celebrating Our Cultural Harvest, by Dorothy Winbush Riley.
First Fruits: The Family Guide to Celebrating Kwanzaa, by Imani Humphrey.
How to Plan a Kwanzaa Celebration: Ideas for Family, Community and Public Events, by Ida Gamble-Bums and Bob Gumbs, Cultural Expressions, Inc., 1998.
Kwanzaa: A Celebration of Family, Community and Culture, by Maulana Karenga, University of Sankore Press, 1997.
Kwanzaa: An African-American Celebration of Culture and Cooking, by Eric V. Copage.

Kwanzaa: An Everyday Resource and Instructional Guide, by David Anderson.

Kwanzaa Crafts: Gifts & Decorations for a Meaningful & Festive Celebration, by Marcia Odle McNair.

Kwanzaa: Everything You Always Wanted to Know but Didn't Know Where to Ask, by Cedric McClester, 30th anniversary edition.

Kwanzaa Karamu: Cooking and Crafts for a Kwanzaa Feast, by April A. Brady.

A Kwanzaa Keepsake, by Jessica B. Harris.

The Nguzo Saba and the Festival of the First Fruits: A Guide for Promoting Family, Community Values and the Celebration of Kwanzaa, by Johnson, Johnson, and Slaughter, Gumbs and Thomas Publishers, Inc., 1995.

Other Adult Books for Gift-Giving

Nonfiction

African American Art and Artists, by Samella Lewis, University of California Press, revised and expanded edition, 2003.

The African-American Century: How Black Americans Have Shaped Our Country, by Henry Louis Gates and Cornel West, Free Press reprint edition, 2002.

African American Wisdom, by Reginald McKnight, New World Library, 2000.

The African Origin of Civilization: Myth or Reality, by Chiek Anta Diop, Lawrence Hill Books, 1974.

African Origins of Major "Western Religions," by Yosef ben Jochannan, Black Classic Press, 1991.

Africans at the Crossroad: Notes on an African World Revolution, by John Henrik Clarke, Africa World Press, 1992.

Afrocentricity: The Theory of Social Change, by Molefi Kete Asante, African American Images, expanded edition, 2003.

The Art of Romare Bearden, by Ruth E. Fine, Harry N. Abrams, 2003.

Assata: An Autobiography, by Assata Shakur, Lawrence Hill Books, 1999.

Autobiography of a People: Three Centuries of African American History Told by Those Who Lived It, by Herb Boyd Anchor, 2000.

The Autobiography of Malcolm X: As Told to Alex Haley, by Malcolm X, Ballantine Books reissue, 1987, with a foreword by Attallah Shabazz.
The Autobiography of Martin Luther King, Jr., by M.L.K. Jr. and Clayborne Carson, Warner Books, reissued, 2001.
Awakening the Natural Genius of Black Children, by Amos Wilson, Afrikan World Infosystems, 1992.
Bearing the Cross: Martin Luther King, Jr. and the Southern Christian Leadership Conference, by David Garrow, Harper Perennial Modern Classics reprint, 2004.
Before the Legend: The Rise of Bob Marley, by Christopher John Farley, Amistad, 2006.
Birth of a Nation'hood: Gaze, Script, and Spectacle in the O. J. Simpson Case, edited by Toni Morrison, Pantheon, 1997.
Black American Cinema, by Manthia Diawara, Routledge, 1993.
The Black Interior, by Elizabeth Alexander, Graywolf Press, 2004.
Black Culture Centers; Politics of Survival and Identity, edited by Fred Lee Hord, Third World Press, 2005.
Black Genius: African-American Solutions to African-American Problems, by multiple editors, Norton, 2000.
Black Man of the Nile and His Family, by Yosef ben Jochannan, Black Classic Press, 1989.
Black Men: Obsolete, Single, Dangerous? The Afrikan American Family in Transition: Essays in Discovery, Solution and Hope, by Haki Madhubuti, Third World Press, 1998.
A Black Parent's Handbook to Educating Your Children (Outside of the Classroom), by Baruti Kafele, Baruti Publishing, 1991.
The Black Woman: An Anthology, by Toni Cade Bambara, Washington Square Press, reprinted, 2005.
Blueprint for Black Power: A Moral, Political, and Economic Imperative for the Twenty-First Century, by Amos Wilson, Afrikan World Infosystems, 1998.
Bob Marley & Peter Tosh Get Up! Stand Up! Diary of a Reggaeophile, by Fikisha Cumbo, Cace International, 2003.
Brothers and Keepers, by John Edgar Wideman, Vintage, 1995.
Christopher Columbus and the Afrikan Holocaust: Slavery and the Rise of European Capitalism, by John Henrik Clarke, A&B Distributors, 2002.

Clarity as Concept: A Poet's Perspective, by Mari Evans, Third World Press, 2006.

The Collected Autobiographies of Maya Angelou, Modern Library, 2004.

Come Hell or High Water: Hurricane Katrina and the Color of Disaster, by Michael Eric Dyson, Perseus Books Group, 2006.

Cornel West and Philosophy (Africana Thought), by Charles Shole Johnson, Routledge, 2002.

The Covenant with Black America, edited by Tavis Smiley, Third World Press, 2006.

The Crisis of the Negro Intellectual, by Harold Cruse, New York Review Classics, 2005.

The Debt: What America Owes to Blacks, by Randall Robinson, Plume, 2001.

Deep Sightings & Rescue Missions: Fiction, Essays, and Conversations, by Toni Cade Bambara, Vintage, 1999.

Democracy Matters: Winning the Fight Against Imperialism, by Cornel West, Penguin Press HC, 2004.

Don't Play in the Sun: One Woman's Journey Through the Color Complex, by Marita Golden, Doubleday, 2004.

Erasing Racism: The Survival of the American Nation, by Molefi Kete Asante, Prometheus Books, 2003.

The Essential Harold Cruse Reader, by William Jelani Cobb, Palgrave Macmillan, 2002.

Every Goodbye Ain't Gone, by Itabari Njeri, Vintage, reprint, 1991.

Eyewitness: A Living Documentary of the African American Contribution to American History, by William Loren Katz, Touchstone, revised, 1995.

Fatheralong, by John Edgar Wideman, Vintage, 1995.

Freedom Dreams: The Black Radical Imagination, by Robin D. G. Kelley, Beacon Press, 2003.

From Slavery to Freedom: A History of African Americas, by John Hope Franklin, Knopf, 2000.

From Superman to Man, by J. A. Rodgers Amereon Limited, 1957 (some online).

The Games Black Girls Play: Learning the Ropes from Double Dutch to Hip-Hop, New York University Press, 2006.

The Gentle Giant: The Autobiography of Yusef Lateef, with Herb Boyd, First Morton Books Edition, 2006.

A Handbook for Teachers of African American Children, by Baruti K. Kafele, Baruti Publishing, 2004.

The House That Race Built: Original Essays by Toni Morrison, Angela Y. Davis, Cornel West, and Others on Black Americans and Politics in America Today, edited by Wahneema Lubiano, Random House, 1998.

How to Plan Your African-American Family Reunion, by Krystal Williams, Citadel Press, 2000.

How I Wrote Jubilee, by Margaret Walker, Third World Press, 1997.

I Know What the Red Clay Looks Like, by Rebecca Carroll, Random House Value Publishing, 1998.

Inner Lives: Voices of African American Women in Prison, by Paula C. Johnson, New York University Press, 2004.

Introduction to Black Studies, by Maulana Karenga (3rd ed.). University of Sankore Press, 2002.

I Write What I Like: Selected Writings, by Steve Biko, University of Chicago Press, 2002.

John Henrik Clarke: The Early Years, by Barbara Eleanor Adams, United Brothers and Sisters, 1992.

Lure and Loathing: Essays on Race, Identity, and the Ambivalence of Assimilation, edited by Gerald Early, Penguin, reprinted, 1994.

Mad at Miles: A Black Woman's Guide to Truth, by Pearl Cleage, Cleage Group, 1990.

Malcolm X: Make It Plain, by William Strickland and Cheryll Y. Greene, Penguin USA, reprint, 1995.

Metu Neter Vol. 1: The Great Oracle of Tehuti and the Egyptian System of Spiritual Cultivation, by Ra Un Nefer Amen, Khamit Media Trans Visions Inc., 1990.

The Middle Passage: White Ships/Black Cargo, by Tom Feelings and John Henrik, Clarke Dial, 1995.

The Miseducation of the Negro, by Carter G. Woodson, Africa World Press, reprinted, 2006.

The Muhammad Ali Reader, edited by Gerald Early, Ecco Press, 1999.

My Life in Search of Africa, by John Henrik Clarke, Third World Press.

My Soul Has Grown Deep: Classics of Early African American Literature, by John Edgar, Wideman Running Press, 2001.

Not the Triumph but the Struggle: 1968 Olympics and the Making of the Black Athlete, by Amy Bass, University of Minnesota Press, 2004.

The Paradox of Loyalty: An African American Response to the War on Terrorism, by Dr. Julianne Malveaux and Reginna A. Green, Third World Press, 2004.

Picturing Us: African American Identity in Photography, by Deborah Willis, New Press, 1996.

Playing in the Dark: Whiteness and the Literary Imagination, by Toni Morrison, Harvard University Press, 1992.

Primer for Blacks, by Gwendolyn Brooks, Third World Press, 1980.

The Prisoner's Wife, by Asha Bandele, Scribner, 2000.

Quitting America: The Departure of a Black Man from His Native Land, by Randall Robinson, Plume, 2004.

Race Woman: The Lives of Shirley Graham Du Bois, Gerald Horne, NYU Press, 2002.

Ready for Revolution: The Life and Struggles of Stokely Carmichael (Kwame Ture), by Stokely Carmichael, Ekwueme Michael Thelwell, and John Edgar Wideman, Scribner, reprint, 2005.

The Rebirth of African Civilization, by Chancellor Williams, Third World Press, 1993.

Role Call: A Generational Anthology of Social and Political Black Literature and Art, edited by Tony Medina, Samiya Bashir, and Quraysh Ali Lansana, Third World Press, 2002.

Seeking the Sakhu: Foundational Writings for an African Psychology, by Wade W. Nobles, Third World Press, 2006.

60 Visions: A Book of Prophecy, by Bob Marley, Tuff Gong Books, 2005.

Swing Low: Black Men Writing, by Rebecca Carroll, Clarkson Potter, 1st edition, 1995.

They Came Before Columbus: The African Presence in Ancient America, by Ivan Van Sertima, Random House, reprint 2003.

The Way of the Elders: West African Spirituality and Tradition, by Adama Doumbia and Naomi Doumbia, Llewellyn Publications, 2004.

We Shall Overcome: The History of the Civil Rights Movement as It Happened (Book with 2 Audio CDs), by Herb Boyd, Sourcebooks Mediafusion, 2004.

When and Where I Enter: The Impact of Black Women on Race and Sex in America, by Paula J. Giddings, Amistad, 1996.

What's My Name, Fool? Sports and Resistance in the United States by Dave Zirin, Haymarket Books, 2005

Willow Weep for Me: A Black Woman's Journey Through Depression, by Meri Nana-Ama Danquah, One World/Ballentine, 1999.
With Ossie and Ruby: In This Life Together, Harper, 2000.
Words to Make My Dream Children Live: A Book of African American Quotations, by Deirdre Mullane, Anchor, 1995.
World's Great Men of Color, Volume I, by J. A. Rogers and John Henrik Clarke Touchstone, revised, 1996.
Yellow Black: The First Twenty-One Years of a Poet's Life, by Haki Madhubuti, Third World Press, 2006.

Novels and Short-Story Collections

American Desert, by Percival Everett, Hyperion, 2004.
Ark of Bones and Other Stories, by Henry Dumas, Random House, 1974.
Babylon Sisters: A Novel, by Pearl Cleage, One World/Ballantine, 2006.
The Between, by Tananarive Due, HarperTorch, 2005.
Blanche on the Lam (and others of the Blanche mysteries), by Barbara Neely, Penguin.
Cane, by Jean Toomer, Liveright, 1993.
The Color Line, by Walker Smith, Sonata Books, April 2005.
Dancing in the Dark, by Caryl Phillips, Knopf, 2005.
Daughter, by Asha Bandele, Scribner, 2004.
The Dew Breaker, by Edwidge Danticat, Vintage, 2005.
The Fall of Rome: A Novel, by Martha Southgate, Scribner, 2002.
Gabriel's Story, by David Anthony Durham, Anchor, 2002.
God's Bits of Wood, by Ousmane Sembene, Heinemann, new edition, 1996.
God's Gym: Stories, by John Edgar Wideman, Mariner Books, reprint, 1998.
In Love and Trouble: Stories of Black Women, by Alice Walker, Harvest Books, 2003.
The Intuitionist: A Novel, by Colson Whitehead, Anchor, 2000.
Invisible Man, by Ralph Ellison, Vintage, 1995.
The Joys of Motherhood, by Buchi Emecheta, George Braziller, 1980.
Jubilee, by Margaret Walker, Mariner Books, reprinted, 1999.
Kindred, by Octavia Butler, Beacon Press, 25th anniversary edition, 2004.
Mama Day, by Gloria Naylor, Vintage, 1989.
The Man in My Basement, by Walter Mosley, Back Bay Books, 2005.

The Man Who Cried I Am, by John A. Williams, Overlook TP, reprinted, 2004.

Measure of Time, by Rosa Guy, Bantam, 1986.

Montgomery's Children: A Novel, by Richard Perry, Genesis Press, 1998.

Parable of the Sower, by Octavia Butler, Rebound by Sagebrush, 1999.

Praisesong for the Widow, by Paule Marshall, Putnam Adult, 1983.

Pushkin and the Queen of Spades: A Novel, by Alice Randall, Houghton-Mifflin, 2004.

Segu, by Maryse Conde, Penguin, 1998.

Shaking the Tree: A Collection of New Fiction and Memoir by Black Women, edited by Meri Nana-Ama Danquah, Norton, 2004.

Sippi: A Novel, by John Oliver Killens, Thunder's Mouth Press, 1988.

Some Things I Never Thought I'd Do, by Pearl Cleage, One World/Ballantine, 2006.

Song of Solomon, by Toni Morrison, Plume Books, 1987.

The Spook Who Sat By the Door, by Sam Greenlee, Lushena Books, 2002.

Their Eyes Were Watching God, by Zora Neale Hurston, Harper, 1998.

Those Bones Are Not My Child, by Toni Cade Bambara, Womens Pr Ltd., new edition, 2001.

When Death Comes Stealing (Tamara Hayle mystery series), by Valerie Wilson Wesley, Avon and One World/Ballantine.

Poetry Books and Collections

The Alphabet Verses: The Ghetto by Jessica Care Moore, Moore Black Press, 2004.

American Smooth, by Rita Dove, Norton, 2006.

The Architecture of Language by Quincy Troupe, Coffee House Press, 2006.

Black Feeling, Black Talk, Black Judgment by Nikki Giovanni, Perennial, 2001.

Black Fire: An Anthology of Afro-American Writing, edited by Amiri Baraka and Larry Neal, Black Classic Press, reissue, 2007.

The Black Poets, edited by Dudley Randall Bantam, reissue, 1985.

Blacks, by Gwendolyn Brooks, Third World Press, 1994.

Blue Lights and River Songs by Tom Dent, Lotus Press, 1982.

Bluestown Mockingbird Mambo by Sandra Maria Esteves, Arte Publico Press, 1990.

Bum Rush the Page: A Def Poetry Jam (anthology), foreword by Sonia Sanchez, edited by Tony Medina and Louis Reyes Rivera, Three Rivers Press, 2001.

Collected Poems, by Robert Earl Hayden, Liveright, 1985.

The Collected Poems of Langston Hughes, Vintage, 1995.

The Dead Emcee Scrolls: The Lost Teachings of Hip-Hop by Saul Williams, MTV Books/Pocket Books, 2006.

Directed by Desire: The Collected Poems of June Jordan Cooper, Canyon Press, 2005.

The Eye in the Ceiling by Eugene B. Redmond, Writers and Readers, 1992.

Groundwork: New and Selected Poems of Don L. Lee/Haki R. Madhubuti from 1966–1996, Third World Press, 1996.

Hoodoo Hollerin' Bebop Ghosts, by Larry Neal, Howard University Press, 1974.

The Moon Is My Witness by Layding Kaliba, Single Action Productions, 1988.

If I Could Sing: Selected Poems, by Keorapetse "Willie" Kgositsile, Kwela Books, 2002.

Most Way Home, by Kevin Young, Zoland Books, 1998.

Poetry for My People, by Henry Dumas, Southern Illinois University Press, 1971.

Scattered Scripture by Louis Reyes Rivera, Shamal Books, 1996.

The Search for Color Everywhere: A Collection of African Poetry, edited by E. Ethelbert Miller, Stewart, Tabori and Chang, new edition, 1996.

Shake Loose My Skin: New and Selected Poems, by Sonia Sanchez, Beacon Press, 2000.

So Far So Good by Gil-Scott Heron, Third World Press, 1990.

Somewhere in Advance of Nowhere, Serpents Tail by Jayne Cortez, 1996.

They Shall Run: Harriet Tubman Poems, by Quraysh Ali Lansana, Third World Press, 2007.

This Is My Century: New and Collected Poems, by Margaret Walker, University of Georgia, 1989.

Un Poco Low Coup, by Amiri Baraka, Reed Cannon & Johnson Pub, 2004.

The Venus Hottentot, by Elizabeth Alexander, Greywolf Press, 2004.

Films for Gift-Giving (on DVD and VHS)

Documentaries

Africa: Open for Business. Entrepreneurial spirit and success on the continent, www.africaopenforbusiness.com.

African American Lives: Discovering Roots. Instructive genealogical journeys using famous people as examples, www.shoppbs.org.

Afro Punk. A frank, funny, and sad documentary on Black punk-rock devotees, www.afropunk.com.

All Power to the People. Electronic Newsgroup, (323) 661-1380, individual distribution only.

Amandla! A Revolution in Four-Part Harmony. Vibrantly examines the role of music in the South African struggle against apartheid.

American Experience: Reconstruction: The Second Civil War. Comprehensive, enlightening, paradigm-changing.

August Wilson: The American Dream in Black and White. Journey of the late playwright, www.films.com.

Badasssss! Mario Van Peebles's take on his dad's making of *Sweet Sweetback*—outrageous!

Baadassss Cinema. By Issac Julien www.accessriverside.com.

The Battle of Algiers. An unflinching assessment of a famous battle for independence.

Beah: A Black Woman Speaks. Directed by Lisa Gay Hamilton, empowering documentary on the actress, www.wmm.org.

Beyond Beats and Rhymes. Addressing manhood in hip hop culture directed by Byron Hurt, www.bhurt.com.

Black Athena. African origins of Greek civilization, by Professor Martin Bernal, newsreel.org.

Black Theater: The Making of a Movement. The birth of new theater from the activism of the 1950s, '60s, and '70s, newsreel.org.

The Black Press, Sweet Honey in the Rock, Jonestown. And others by Stanley Nelson, www.firelightmedia.org.

Black Wax. A 1982 documentary on Gil Scott Heron by Robert Mugge.

Brother Outsider: The Life of Bayard Rustin. The organizer of the March on Washington suffered as an openly gay man, newsreel.org.

Chisolm 72: Unbought and Unbossed. By Shola Lynch, important and enjoyable film.

Classified X. Melvin Van Peebles on the representation of Blacks in film.

Congo: White King, Red Rubber, Black Death. Documentary on brutal colonialism in the Congo.

Darwin's Nightmare. Disturbing, important doc on results of altering the food supply in an African nation.

Deadline. Illinois governor considers fate of death row prisoners before leaving office.

Dead Prez: It's Bigger than Hip-Hop. The music and the issues, directed by John Threat, www.starz.com.

Eyes on the Prize series. Consummate documentary on the Civil Rights Movement, 1952 to 1965.

4 Little Girls. Moving documentary on the bombing of a Birmingham church by Southern racists.

Free to Dance. The influence of Black choreographers on American dance, www.nbpc.tv.

Furious Flower II: The Black Poetic Tradition. Great performances and the origins of contemporary Black poetry, newsreel.org.

A Great Day in Harlem. Documentary on the making of the famous photo and the jazz musicians in it.

Hoop Dreams. Award-winning doc on two young basketball players scouted by an elite white school.

How to Eat Your Watermelon in White Company and Enjoy It. Interesting doc on the salty and frenetically creative filmmaker Melvin Van Peebles.

Ida B. Wells: A Passion for Justice. Great doc on the antilynching journalist, with Toni Morrison, www.williamgreaves.com.

In Search of History: The Night Tulsa Burned. History Channel doc on the Black Wall Street destroyed by white rioters.

James Baldwin: The Price of the Ticket. Life and work of the gifted, pained, and passionate novelist and essayist, newsreel.org.

John Henrik Clarke: A Great and Mighty Walk. By St. Clair Bourne, info@cinemaguild.org

The Language You Cry In. Fascinating survival of African culture among African Americans, newsreel.org.

Malcolm X Make It Plain. A PBS "American Experience" film directed by Orlando Bagwell.

Music Is My Life, Politics, My Mistress: The Oscar Brown Jr. Story. Donnie

L. Betts, director/producer, another must-have, www.musicismy life.info.

No! Aishah Shahidah Simmons, survivors of sexual assault, www.notherapedocumentary.org.

Nat Turner: A Troublesome Property. About the leader of a famous slave rebellion, directed by Charles Burnett, newsreel.org.

Negroes with Guns: Rob Williams and Black Power. He opened a new chapter in the struggle against Jim Crow, newsreel.org.

Nina Simone: Love Sorceress. Directed by Rene Letzgus.

A Panther in Africa. A former Black Panther living for decades in Africa, www.apantherinafrica.com.

Public Enemy. Uncommonly objective look at the Black Panther Party, directed by Jens Meurer.

Race: The Power of an Illusion. A three-part series that tackles the notion of race as a biological reality, newsreel.org.

Race to Execution. Race and the death penalty, www.filmakers .com/in-divs/RaceExecution.htm.

Ralph Bunche: An American Odyssey. Directed by William Greaves and narrated by Sidney Poitier.

Ralph Ellison: An American Journey. Narrated by Andre Braugher with a roster of literary greats, newsreel.org.

The Untold Story of Emmett Louis Till. Documentary by Keith A. Beauchamp, tillfreedomcome@aol.com.

Toni Morrison. In her own words and hypnotic reading, Morrison addresses slavery, Homevision, 2000.

Unforgivable Blackness: The Rise and Fall of Jack Johnson. Absorbing examination of the conflicts and context, www.shoppbs.org.

Voices of the Gods, Durban 400, A Litany for Survival. Three great films by gifted independent filmmaker Al Santana, www.twn.org.

W.E.B. Du Bois: A Biography in Four Voices. Brilliant film by Louis Massiah, with Toni Cade Bambara, Wesley Brown, etc., newsreel.org.

When the Levees Broke: A Requiem in Four Acts. Spike Lee's masterful documentary on the victims of Hurricane Katrina.

Wild Women Don't Have the Blues. The lives and times of great blues singers such as Rainey, Smith, and Waters, newsreel.org.

Features

Antwoine Fisher. True story of a young man who's helped to overcome his painful history.

Bamboozled. Spike Lee's controversial film about modern-day minstrelsy.

Ceddo, Xala, Moolade. And other must-see films by master Ousmane Sembene.

The Court-Martial of Jackie Robinson. Dramatization of the little-known history of the icon's life before baseball.

Cooley High. Generations adore this comedy/drama with Glynn Turman and Lawrence Hilton-Jacobs.

Cosmic Slop. A Twilight Zone–type trio of stories addressing Black identity and other issues.

Daughters of the Dust. A groundbreaking and visually rich film written and directed by Julie Dash.

Down in the Delta. Directed by Maya Angelou, with Alfre Woodard, Wesley Snipes, Mary Alice, and others.

Eve's Bayou. Haunting and beautifully shot tale of a young girl in a dysfunctional family.

The Five Heartbeats. This favorite tells the story of the rise and fall of a fictional sixties singing group.

The Flip Wilson Show. Another groundbreaking comedy/variety TV show.

For Love of Ivy. Sidney Poitier and Abbey Lincoln bring captivating magic to a negligible plot.

Glory. Tells the true story of the 54th Regiment of Black soldiers in the Civil War.

The Healing Passage: Voices from the Water. The reverberations of the African Holocaust in the lives of people of African descent, www.asharpshow.com/shop_page_2.htm.

Hollywood Shuffle. Humorous look at the plight of Black actors in Hollywood.

Hotel Rwanda. Wrenching and important, based on the true story of heroism amid the massacre.

The Hurricane. Based on the story of Ruben "Hurricane" Carter, a boxer wrongly imprisoned for murder.

The Keeper. Directed by Joe Brewster, interesting story addresses class issues in the Black community.

Lumumba, Sometimes in April, Haitian Corner. Visceral biography and fact-based dramas by Raoul Peck.

Maangamizi. African American psychiatrist working in a Tanzanian asylum has her paradigm shifted, www.grisgrisfilms.com/html/store.html.

Nothin' But a Man. A loving couple face the racism of the early 1960s. Stars Ivan Dixon and Abbey Lincoln.

One Love. Richly visual Jamaican love story addressing contemporary issues, www.coloroffilm.com.

The Piano Lesson. TV-movie adaptation of August Wilson's play.

Posse. Action-packed Black western, directed by Mario Van Peebles.

Putney Swope. Controversial (in 1969) comedy in which a Black man takes over an ad agency.

Quilombo. This film depicts the seventeenth-century uprising of enslaved Africans in Brazil.

A Raisin in the Sun. Wonderful adaptation of Lorraine Hansberry's masterful play, with Sidney Poitier and Ruby Dee.

The Richard Pryor Show. This TV variety show was another example of Pryor's comic genius.

The River Niger. James Earl Jones and Cicely Tyson star in this adaptation of the off-Broadway hit.

Rosewood. Gripping film based on the true story of a 1920s racist attack on a Florida town.

Sankofa, Adwa, Wilmington 10, Ashes and Embers. And other films by Haile Gerima.

Something the Lord Made. Based on the true story about an unsung heart surgery pioneer.

Sparkle. The classic 1976 forerunner to *Dreamgirls,* with Lonette McKee and Irene Cara.

The Spook Who Sat by the Door. Wild political comedy that's become a cult classic.

To Sleep with Anger. A classic Charles Burnett drama: dark, funny, true, with Danny Glover, Mary Alice, etc.

Tsotsi. A violent Johannesburg gang leader is transformed when has to care for an infant.

White Man's Burden. Flawed, but original drama/satire in which Blacks are elites and whites underprivileged.

X. Spike Lee's biopic on the great leader and orator.

Family Films

Amazing Grace. Directed by Stan Lathan with Moms Mabley and Rosalind Cash.

The Autobiography of Miss Jane Pittman, 30th Anniversary Edition. Stars Cicely Tyson, from the Ernest J. Gaines book, www.shoppbs.org.

Buck and the Preacher. Sidney Poitier directs and stars (with Belafonte) in this Black heritage/adventure Western.

Bingo Long Traveling All-Stars and Motor Kings. Great comedy about an enterprising Negro League baseball player, Billy Dee Williams

Boycott. Superior film on the Montgomery Bus Boycott. Great cast and novel approach.

Claudine. Stars Diahann Carroll and James Earl Jones, with a soundtrack by Curtis Mayfield.

Cool Runnings. Great comedy based on the true story of the Jamaican Olympic bobsled team.

Cornbread, Earl and Me. Touching coming-of-age classic; a plotline tragedy may be disturbing to young children.

Five on the Black Hand Side. This 1970s comedy aimed to instill Black pride amid the flurry of Blaxploitation films.

The Gift of Amazing Grace. Musical about a young girl and her talent.

Gullah, Gullah Island This 1990s Nick Jr. series features a Black family and friends, music, puppets, and more.

Having Our Say: The Delany Sisters' First 100 Years. The life and times of two super seniors, based on a true story, a book, and Broadway play.

House of Dies Drear. Runaway slaves haunt an old house, based on the Virginia Hamilton novel.

Jump In! Young boxer discovers his hidden talent in a Double Dutch competition.

Kirkou and the Sorceress. An African boy born with magical powers defends his village from an evil sorceress.

The Last Dragon. Over-the-top, fun Black martial arts movie; teens may like it, but not admit it.

Lean on Me. Based on the real-life Joe Clark, a tough-love school principle.

The Learning Tree. A classic coming-of-age film written and directed by the legendary Gordon Parks.

Nightjohn. Beautifully shot family feature with an important historical angle, by Charles Burnett.

Once Upon a Time When We Were Colored. Family film directed by Tim Reid.

Rabbit-Proof Fence. Heroic true story of three young Aborigine girls kidnapped by the government.

Race to Freedom: The Underground Railroad. A group of slaves risk their lives to follow Harriet Tubman to freedom.

The Rosa Parks Story. Wonderful direction by Julie Dash and acting by Angela Bassett.

Ruby Bridges. Based on the true story of a young girl who helped to integrate New Orleans schools.

Sarafina! Musical about a South African resilient girl living under the Apartheid regime.

Sirga (L'Enfant Lion). Beautiful, awe-inspiring film about twin spirits—a boy and a lion.

Sounder. Cicely Tyson and Paul Winfield head a strong, proud family of sharecroppers.

Stand and Deliver! Classic about a teacher who refused to give up on his underperforming students.

Sugar Cane Alley. Powerful classic written and directed by Euzhan Palcy.

Whale Rider. Maori girls fulfills her destiny and helps her village by standing up for herself.

The Wiz. Film adaptation of the Black Broadway musical based on The Wizard of Oz.

A Woman Called Moses. Stars Cicely Tyson and written by Lonne Elder III.

Independent Film Festivals, Organizations, and Resources

African Diaspora Film Festival. www.nyadff.org.
African Family Film Foundation. Shorts on music and culture, made in Africa, www.africanfamily.org/films.html.
The Black Documentary Collective. Networking, education, collective promotion, and screenings, www.bdcny.net.
Black Man Film Festival. www.afrikan.net/hype.
Film commentary and interviews. www.seeingblack.com.
Harlem Film Festival. www.harlemfilmfestival.com/default.shtml.
Imagenation Film and Music Festival. Free screenings, distributes films. www.imagenation.us/pages/main.htm.
The International Black Panther Film Festival. www.pantherfilmfest.com/index.html.
National Black Programming Consortium. Provides quality docs to public TV, www.nbpc.tv.
Public Broadcasting Service. Purchase copies of *American Experience, Civil Rights,* and other series, www.pbs.org.
Reel Sisters of the Diaspora Film Festival and Lecture Series. www.reelsisters.org.
San Francisco Black Film Festival. www.sfbff.org.
Texas Black Film Festival. texasblackfilmfestival.com.
Third World Newsreel. Thousands of films to buy or rent, (212) 947-9277, www.twn.org.

Sources for Kwanzaa Table Items, Gifts, Decorating, and Attire

Barbados

Roots and Grasses (beautiful baskets). 23 Pelican Village, Harbour Road, (246) 431-0588, www.rootsandgrasses.com.

Canada

Ashanti Room. 836 Bloor Street West, Toronto, (416) 588-3934, www.ashantiroom.com.

Burke's Books. 873 St. Clair Avenue West, Toronto, (416) 656-5366.

A Different Booklist. 746 Bathurst Street, Toronto, (416) 538-0889, www.adifferentbooklist.com.

Knowledge Bookstore. 177 Queen Street West, Brampton, Ontario, (905) 459-9875, www.knowledgebookstore.com.

England

Headstart Books and Crafts. 25 West Green Road, London, 020 8802 2838.

Mama Arika Kulcha Shap. 282 High Road Leyton, London, 020 8539 2154.

YEMANJA—A Window to Afrika. 446 Birchfield Road, Perry Barr, Birmingham, 0121 344 3744, www.yemanjaonline.com.

France

Louse Balances (African fabrics). 36 rue Polonceau, Paris.

Jamaica

Headstart Books & Crafts.
54 Church Street, Jamaica, West Indies, (876) 922-3915.

New Zealand

Kwanzaa—The Afrikan Shop (crafts, gifts, Kwanzaa kits, info, and celebration) 119 Manners Street, Wellington, 04 801 7773, sunflower@actrix.co.nz.

United States

The following businesses are located across the United States and most have websites from which their products can be purchased.

Kwanzaa Table Materials, Crafts, and Related

African City Alive! 2121A St. Francis, Palo Alto, California, (650) 856-8335, www. africancityalive.com.

Complete Kwanzaa Kit.
www.meekwanzaakit.com.

Doretha's African-American Books & Gifts.
5410 Two Notch Road, Suite D,
Columbia, South Carolina, (803) 782-9833.

An electric kinara!
www.kwanzaalights.com/kinarainfo.htm.

Eman Fine Art. (905) 544-2244, www.emanarts.com.

Fatou Touba Mbacke.
Malcolm Shabazz Harlem Market, West 115th Street at Lenox Avenue, Booth 43, New York City, (917) 517-5407.

Headstart Books & Crafts, Inc. P.O Box 682167, Orlando, Florida, (407) 814-2665, info@headstartbooks.com.

Karibu Gifts in California.
427 Water Street, Jack London Square, Oakland, California, (510) 444-6906.

Kinara, arts, and handmade crafts. Carmen Seldon, (609) 851-6436.

Kinara, candles, kikombe, and bowl. dfbgcards.com/designsforbetter-giving/kwanzaa/kwanzaa.htm.l

Source International Technology Corporation. Distributes multicultural books and the Black Fax Calendar,
Bronx, New York, (718) 378-3878, www.nal.net/sourceintl.

Ulinzi wa Uungwana Enterprises
Fabrics and crafts from Tanzania; founder Mteteaji Milimwengu also leads Kwanzaa ceremonies for hire, swahili-man@webtv.net.

Kwanzaa and Other Greeting Cards

Beautiful art cards for all occasions. dfbgcards.com/home.

Beautiful collage, painted, and illustrated cards.
(718) 485-8507, saharkardz@yahoo.com.

Cards, invitations, journals, and more.
Carole Joy Creations, Inc., www.carolejoy.com.

Great cards in some new styles.
www.thegreetingcardman.com.

Lovely original art cards.
www.artfulgreetings.com.

A nice selection and note cards, too.
www.beautifullyblack.com/notes/notes.asp.

Young, urban, and inspirational.
www.bigupdesign.com.

Clothing and Accessories

African print fabrics.
www.afritex.com.

Afri-Ware Inc.
948 Lake Street, Oak Park, Illinois, (708) 524-8398.

Beautiful and unusual beadwork.
(212) 491-6726, www.shimoda-accessories.com.

Cultural gift items and clothing.
4W Circle of Art & Enterprise, (718) 876-6500, www.4wcircle.com.

Exquisite wearable art handbags.
www.marvinsin.com.

If you're into ankhs . . . www.cafepress.com/allankh.

Ingeniously styled straw and cloth hats.
Matthew's Hats, (718) 859-4683, www.matthewshats.com.

Inspired clothing and jewelry design.
DeFaybe, (917) 701-9864, www.denisebeckford.com.

Popular African-inspired designer.
Moshood, www.afrikanspirit.com.

Sterling silver in authentic African styles.
Fine Silver by Efua and Nana, www.efuasilver.com.

Strapak organizer frontpack.
Tarik Karenga's original design (Maulana Karenga's son), www.tarikkarenga.com/products.html.

Taking it to the brim: more great straw.
www.hatsbybunn.com.

Wearable art.
Tribal Truths Collection by Brenda Brunson-Bey, (718) 643-8322.

Art, Home Furnishings, and Home Accessories

Africa by the Bay. Oakland, California, (510) 763-8000, www.africabythebay.com (click on ONLINE STORE).

African cultural items at Sisa'rt.
11115 50th Avenue, South Tukwila, Washington, (206) 722-2381.

African culture and Black history wall calendars.
www.cafepress.com/africalendars/1106275.

Art illustrations and posters. (917) 206-3613, onajeasheber@hotmail.com.

Artistic handmade quilts.
www.myrahbrowngreen.com.

Art prints, figurines, mugs, and more.
www.ebonyart.com.

Art to enliven the home, illustration.
Jimmy James Greene, jimmyjamesgreene@hotmail.com.

Black Artists of DC. See the work of artists in the nation's capital, blackartistsofdc.org.

Chester Higgins. Fabulous online gallery and gorgeous photo books, including: "Feeling the Spirit," "Elder Grace," and others, www.chester higgins.com.

Copper relief art and paintings. Miriam B. Francis, (718) 855-2118.

Cultural gift items in Seattle. Nya's Notion, 8850 24th Avenue SW, Seattle, Washington, (206) 380-5753.

A different kinara, masks, and other gifts.
www.thegreetingcardman.com.

Gifts and crafts for the home.
www.zawadigiftshop.com.

Lovely oil paintings and illustrations.
Ann Tanksley, www.artnet.com.

Lovely painting and collage.
ramonacandy.com.

National Conference of Artists.
See Black artists' work and contact them nationwide,
(212) 420-7892, www.ncanewyork.com.

An online source for readers.
www.africanbookstore.net/default.asp.

Oregon shop for African cultural gift choices. Folami's Gifts, PO Box 6242, Beaverton, Oregon 97007, (503) 992-2188.

Yú—Accessories for Modern Living. Fine furniture and home-related gifts, Fort Greene, Brooklyn, (718) 237-5878.

Gift-Subscription Ideas

African American Review. An archive of scholarly journals, www.jstor.org.

African Voices Magazine. Literary, visual, and other arts and events, www.africanvoices.com.

American Legacy. African-American history and culture, www.americanlegacymag.com/index.html.

Bfm. Black film, music, and media magazine, www.bfmmedia.com.

The Black Collegian. Career and self-development for students, www.black-collegian.com/news.

Black Enterprise. Long-running Black business monthly magazine.

Black Issues Book Review. Covering authors and publishers for readers, www.bibookreview.com.

The Black Scholar. A journal of Black studies and research, www.theblackscholar.org.

Footsteps Magazine. No longer in print, this valuable magazine for young people offers its catalog of back issues for order via www.footstepsmagazine.com/.

The Network Journal. A Black business monthly magazine, www.tnj.com.

Nka Journal of Contemporary African Art. Critical discourse on African and Diaspora art, www.nkajournal.org.

Solo Mommy Magazine. A publication for Black single mothers, www.solomommy.com.

Souls. Columbia University African-American studies quarterly.

Museums and Galleries

Support by visiting. Many have gift shops.

California African American Museum.
600 State Drive, Exposition Park, Los Angeles, (213) 744-7432, Caa-museum.org.

Corridor Gallery.
334 Grand Avenue, Brooklyn, (718) 638-8416, thecorridorgallery.org.

DuSable Museum of African American History.
740 East 56th Place, Chicago, Illinois, (773) 947-0600, www.dusablemuseum.org.

Hamilton Landmark Galleries
467 West 144th Street, New York City,
(212) 281-7667, www.hamiltonlandmark@hotmail.com.

Hammonds House Galleries and Resource Center.
Fine arts of the African Diaspora, in Atlanta, Georgia,
(404) 752-8730, www.hammondshouse.org.

Hampton University Museum.
Hampton, Virginia (on campus), (757) 727-5308, www.hamptonu.edu/museum.

Howard University Gallery of Art.
2455 6th Street Washington, DC, (202) 806-6111,
www.howard.edu/library/Art@Howard/GoA/default.htm.

Kenkeleba House Gallery.
214 East Second Street, New York City, (212) 229-1890.

Project Row Houses.
2500 Holman Street, Houston, Texas, (713) 526-7662.

Schomburg Center for Research in Black Culture.
515 Malcolm X Boulevard, (212) 491-2200, www.nypl.org/research/sc/sc.html.

Studio Museum in Harlem.
144 West 125th Street, (212) 864-4500, Studiomuseum.org.

Tubman African American Museum.
340 Walnut Street, Macon, Georgia, (478) 743-8544, Tubman museum.com.

Historical, Media, and Other Information Resources

African American history challenge.
www.brightmoments.com/blackhistory.

African ancestored genealogy.
afrigeneas.com/.

African Studies Center at the University of Pennsylvania.
www.africa.upenn.edu/AS.html.

Afro-Cuban cultural and historical info.
afrocubaweb.com.

Alternative news and other radio programming across the United States.
www.pacifica.org.

Arts, media, and politics.
www.seeingblack.com/index.shtml.

Association for the Study of Classical African Civilizations (ASCAC). National and international conferences, www.ascac.org.

Beautiful photos and info on African societies and customs.
www.africawrites.com.

Black Classic Press.
www.blackclassicbooks.com/servlet/StoreFront.

The Black Commentator.
A weekly online Internet magazine, www.blackcommentator.com.

Black Press USA.
News and directory: Black newspapers across the United States, www.blackpressusa.com.

The Black World Today.
A trusted and uncompromising online newspaper, www.tbwt.org.

Chickenbones: An Online Literary Journal.
www.nathanielturner.com/index.html.

Concerned Black Men National Organization.
www.cbmnational.org.

Council of Independent Black Institutions.
Independent schools nationwide. www.cibi.org.

Informative radio with quality Black programs.
Listen online, www.wbai.org.

Info on Africa for teachers.
www.africa.upenn.edu/Home_Page/AFR_GIDE.html.

Joint Center for Political and Economic Studies.
Lots of info on African Americans, www.jointcenter.org.

Like It Is.
Superb and decades-old Black issues and history TV, 7online.com.

Listen to slave narratives.
xroads.virginia.edu/~HYPER/wpa/wpahome.html

Online Academy of the Smithsonian's Anacostia Museum.
anacostia.si.edu/Online_Academy/academy.htm.

Roots Music Karamu
Five years of playlists, Black Diasporan music, www.etvradio.org or OseiTerry@aol.com.

Schomburg Collection for Research in Black Culture.
The motherlode! www.nypl.org/research/sc/sc.html.

TV One Black-owned subscriber-based station
Sometimes shows classic movies, www.tv-one.tv.

Weekly online news and issues journal.
www.blackagendareport.com.

XM 169 The Power 24-hour Black talk radio station, (866) 801-TALK (toll-free), thepower@xmradio.com.

Cultural Festivals, Conferences, and Events

African Street Festival (Society for African-American Cultural Awareness) T. R. White Sportsplex, 304 North Hays Avenue, Jackson, Tennessee,
www.saaca.com.

Black Freedom Weekend.
Richmond, Virginia, happilynaturalday.com/about.htm.

DanceAfrica. Annual weekend festivals in New York City, Chicago, and Washington D.C., bam.org, danceplace.org, and www.colum.edu.

Down Home Family Reunion (A Celebration of African American Folklife). Richmond, Virginia, www.elegbafolkloresociety.org/efs_festivals.html.

Gullah Celebration. www.gullahcelebration.com.

Harlem Week.
harlemweek.harlemdiscover.com/.

International African Arts Festival.
Brooklyn, New York, June–July, www.iaafestival.org.

Juneteenth celebrations nationwide.
www.juneteenth.com.

National Black Arts Festival.
Atlanta, www.nbaf.org/.

National Black Fine Arts Show.
www.nationalblackfineartshow.com/.

National Black Theater Festival.
Durham, North Carolina, www.nbtf.org.

National Black Writers Conference.
Medgar Evers College, Brooklyn, New York, www.mec.cuny.edu/nbwc.

Odunde African American Festival Weekend.
Philadelphia, www.odundeinc.org.

Tribute to the Ancestors (People of the Sun Middle Passage Collective). Coney Island Beach, Brooklyn, New York, poscollective.tripod.com.

Live Dance and Music

Contact information is provided below for a sampling of dance companies and music ensembles in various locales. Most tour and are available for bookings if you're part of an organization planning a large Kwanzaa gathering. Many African dance companies will feature instrumental interludes to showcase the talents of their musicians, so audiences are treated to both music and dance. Practice Ujamaa by supporting working artists when you can. Check the touring schedules of these and other groups and plan to catch them when they come to town. Also, if you're fortunate enough to live where a great dance company is based, remember that most of them conduct dance classes to meet their expenses, so you can help out while getting a good workout.

African American Dance Ensemble.
Durham, North Carolina, (919) 560-2729, www.africanamericandanceensemble.org.

African dance and drum classes throughout Los Angeles.
www.africanbeat.com.

African Dimensions Collective.
Does a full Kwanzaa ceremony with music and dance, New York City, (718) 3767, www.africandimensions.com/kwanzaa.htm.

The Art of Black Dance and Music.
West Somervile, Massachusetts, (617) 666-1859, www.abdm.net.

Asase Ya.
New York City, (718) 462-1101, nsuobri@aol.com.

Balance Dance Theatre.
New York City, www.obediahwright.com/the_stage.html, PelzerMega1@aol.com.

Batoto Yetu.
Children's African dance company,
Harlem, New York, (646) 240-4161, www.batotoyetu.com.

Brilho De Luz Band (Brazil-Brooklyn Connection).
Music and capoeira, www.brilhodeluzband.com.

COBA Collective of Black Artists.
Toronto, Canada, 416 658 3111, www.cobainc.com.

Cleo Parker Robinson Dance Company.
Denver, Colorado, (303) 295-1759, www.cleoparkerdance.org.

Cleveland Contemporary Dance Theatre.
Cleveland, Ohio, (212) 791-9000, www.ccdt.com/main.html.

Coyaba Dance Theater.
Washington D.C., (202) 269-1600, www.danceplace.org/coyaba.

Dallas Black Dance Theatre.
Dallas, Texas, (214) 871-2376, www.dbdt.com.

Dimensions Dance Theatre.
Oakland, California, (510) 465-3363, www.dimensionsdance.org.

Evidence.
Brooklyn, New York, (718) 230-4633, www.evidencedance.com.

Farafina Kan—The Sound of Africa.
Washington D.C., (202) 286.2688, www.farafinakan.com.

Ishangi Family African Dancers.
Travels nationwide, (703) 764-0180, www.ishangi1@aol.com.

Kankouran West African Dance Company.
Washington D.C., (202) 518-1213, www.kankouran.org.

Kulumele African American Dance Company.
Philadelphia, Pennsylvania, (267) 252-6366, www.kulumele.org.

Kuumba House Dance Theatre.
Houston, Texas, (713) 524-1079, www.kuumbahouse.org/home.htm.

Maimouna Keita.
Brooklyn, New York, (646) 852-3009, www.maimounakeita.com.

Mamadou Dahoue and the Ancestral Messengers.
Brooklyn, New York, (917) 291-5333.

Moor Hips.
Bellydancing—the art and the history,
Washington, D.C., (202) 545-8888, gomamasita.com/wst_page6.html.

The Moving Form.
Jazz, poetry, and live visual art,
New York City, (718) 925-0298.

Muntu Dance Theatre of Chicago.
(773) 602-1135, www.muntu.com.

The Nigerian Talking Drum Ensemble.
Los Angeles, California, (323) 294-7445, www.nitade.com.

Niancho Eniyaley West African Dance & Drum.
Duarte, California, (626) 357-3069.

Nzinga Dance.
London, England, 0208 314 5328, www.nzingadance.org.uk/index. htm.

Philidanco.
Philadelphia, Pennsylvania, (215) 387-8200, www.philadanco.org.

Restoration Dance Theatre.
An accomplished children's company,

Brooklyn, New York, (718) 230-0693, www.restorationplaza.org/index.htm.

Rennie Harris Puremovement.
Philadelphia, Pennsylvania, (215) 665-5718, www.rhpm.org.

Silimbo D'Adeane Dance and Drum Company.
Cambridge, Massachusetts, (617) 427-5160, www.silimbo.com.

Songhai Djeli.
Musicians and poets,
New York City, www.songhaidjeli.com.

Sounds of Afrika Drum and Dance.
Danbury, Connecticut, (914) 419-6438, www.soundsofafrika.com.

Step Afrika!
Washington D.C., (202) 462-2595, www.stepafrika.org/home.htm.

Umoja Dance Company.
Montclair, New Jersey, (973) 783-5337, www.umoja dance.com.

Urban Bush Women.
Brooklyn, New York, (718) 398-4537, www.urbanbushwomen.org/home.

Veronica White.
Musician and arranger,
New York City, (718) 467-7631, sistervv@verizonmail.com.

WADaBo—West African Dance in Boston.
Classes in Massachusetts and Vermont, (202) 269-1600, www.wadabo.com.

Appendix

A Glossary and Pronunciation Key

Ase (ah-SHAY) A Yoruba word for intrinsic spiritual power from the one life force.

Bendera (ben-DEH-rah) The red, black, and green flag.

Berimbau (BEH-rim-bau) A Brazilian string instrument played with a bow.

Callaloo (cah-la-LOO) A green, leafy vegetable grown and cooked in the Caribbean.

Futari (foo-TAH-ree) A West African dish made of squash, yams, and coconut milk.

Harambee (hah-rahm-BAY) "All pull together!"

Imani (ee-MAH-nee) Faith (the Seventh Principle).

Joloff Rice (JOE-lof) A popular African dish made with meat or fish and tomato sauce.

Karamu (kah-RAH-moo) Kwanzaa feast, a gathering with music, dedications, etc.

Karenga, Maulana (Kah-RAYN-gah, Mah-oo-LAH-nah) The creator of Kwanzaa.

Kawaida (kah-wah-EE-dah) Maulana Karenga's doctrine of "tradition and reason."

Kente (KEN-teh) A colorful woven cloth originating in Ghana, West Africa.

Kikombe cha Umoja (kee-KOHM-bay cha oo-MOH-jah) The unity cup.

Kinara (kee-NAH-rah) The candleholder.

Kujichagulia (koo-gee-cha-goo-LEE-ah) Self-determination (the Second Principle).

Kuumba (koo-OOM-bah) Creativity (the sixth principle).

Kwanzaa (KWAN-zah) A meaningful holiday created by a person of African descent.

Maafa (mah-AH-fah) The African Holocaust, particularly of enslavement.

Marimba (mah-RIM-bah) A melodic percussion instrument from South Africa.

Matunda ya Kwanzaa (mah-TOON-dah yah KWAN-zah) Celebration of the First Fruits.

Mazao (mah-ZOW, as in "wow") Produce: fruits and vegetables.

Mishumaa Saba (mee-SHOO-mah SAH-bah) The seven candles.

Mkeka (mm-KEH-kah) A mat of woven straw that's placed on the Kwanzaa table.

Muhindi (mu-HIN-dee) Ears of corn placed on the Kwanzaa table.

Nguzo Saba (n-GOO-zo sah-bah) The Seven Principles of Kawaida and Kwanzaa.

Nia (NEE-ah) Purpose (the Fifth Principle).

Oware (oh-WAH-ree) A 7,000-year-old pit-and-pebbles board game from Africa.

Shekere (SHEH-keh-reh) A musical instrument made from a dried gourd.

Tiébou dienn (Cheh-boo JEN) A fish and vegetable dish from Senegal.

Ugali (oo-GAH-lee) An East African corn-flour grain served with various dishes.

Ujamaa (oo-jah-MAH) Cooperative economics (the Fourth Principle).

Ujima (oo-GEE-mah) Collective work and responsibility (the Third Principle).

Umkhosi (um-KOH-see) Traditional Zulu harvest festival.

Umoja (oo-MOH-jah) Unity (the First Principle).

Vibunzi (vee-BOON-zee) Another name for muhindi.

Wimbo (WIM-bo) "Song" in the Kiswahili language.

Zawadi (zah-WAH-dee) "Gift" in the Kiswahili language.

Zom (zohm) A greens-and-peanut dish made in Cameroon.